PATHWAYS TO PURE POWER

Learning the Depth of Love's Power

A Study of 1 Corinthians

Jack W. Hayford
with
Gary Curtis

THOMAS NELSON PUBLISHERS
Nashville

CONTENTS

● ●

Pathways to Pure Power: Learning the Depth of Love's Power (A Study of 1 Corinthians) is one of a series of study guides that focus exciting, discovery-geared coverage of Bible book and power themes—all prompting toward dynamic, Holy Spirit-filled living.

About the Executive Editor

JACK W. HAYFORD, noted pastor, teacher, writer, and composer, is the Executive Editor of the complete series, working with the publisher in the conceiving and developing of each of the books.

Dr. Hayford is Senior Pastor of The Church On The Way, the First Foursquare Church of Van Nuys, California. He and his wife, Anna, have four married children, all of whom are active in either pastoral ministry or vital church life. As General Editor of the *Spirit-Filled Life Bible*, Pastor Hayford led a four-year project, which has resulted in the availability of one of today's most practical and popular study Bibles. He is author of more than twenty books, including *A Passion for Fullness, The Beauty of Spiritual Language, Rebuilding the Real You*, and *Prayer Is Invading the Impossible*. His musical compositions number over four hundred songs, including the widely sung "Majesty."

About the Writer

GARY CURTIS is the Executive Director of Living Way Ministries, the broadcast/media ministry department of The Church On The Way in Van Nuys, California. He administrates an outreach that both daily (radio) and weekly (television) is aired on more than 180 broadcast facilities. His experience as a gifted administrator and pastor has been gained through his involvement in public ministry for over twenty-five years, having served at Illinois' great Moline Gospel Temple with Dr. Charles Hollis and at LIFE Bible College in Los Angeles as Executive Assistant to the President.

He is a graduate of LIFE Bible College, where he was also Student Body President. Graduate studies have been advanced at Fuller Theological Seminary (Pasadena) and at Wheaton Graduate School of Theology and Trinity Evangelical Divinity School in Illinois.

Gary and Alisa Curtis have been married for twenty-six years and have two daughters, Carmen and Coleen, who are both married.

Of this contributor, the Executive Editor has remarked: "I know of no one with a steadier, more reliable pattern of service to Christ than Gary Curtis. His trustworthiness and efficiency bring a quality of depth and integrity to everything he does, whether in the study of the Word or his overseeing of demanding administrative detail."

THE GIFT
THAT KEEPS ON GIVING

Who doesn't like presents? Whether they come wrapped in colorful paper and beautiful bows, or brown paper bags closed and tied at the top with old shoestring. Kids and adults of all ages love getting and opening presents.

But even this moment of surprise and pleasure can be marked by dread and fear. All it takes is for these words to appear: "Assembly Required. Instructions Enclosed." How we hate these words! They taunt us, tease us, beckon us to try to challenge them, all the while knowing that they have the upper hand. If we don't understand the instructions, or if we ignore them and try to put the gift together ourselves, more than likely we'll only assemble frustration and anger. What we felt about our great gift—all the joy, anticipation, and wonder—will vanish. And they will never return, at least not to that pristine state they had before we realized that *we* had to assemble our present with instructions *no consumer* will ever understand.

One of the most precious gifts God has given us is His Word, the Bible. Wrapped in the glory and sacrifice of His Son and delivered by the power and ministry of His Spirit, it is a treasured gift—one the family of God has preserved and protected for centuries as a family heirloom. It promises that it is the gift that keeps on giving, because the Giver it reveals is inexhaustible in His love and grace.

Tragically, though, fewer and fewer people, even those who number themselves among God's everlasting family, are opening this gift and seeking to understand what it's all about and how to use it. They often feel intimidated by it. It requires some assembly, and its instructions are hard to comprehend sometimes. How does the Bible fit together anyway?

What does Genesis have to do with Revelation? Who are Abraham and Moses, and what is their relationship to Jesus and Paul? And what about the works of the Law and the works of faith? What are they all about, and how do they fit together, if at all?

And what does this ancient Book have to say to us who are looking toward the twenty-first century? Will taking the time and energy to understand its instructions and to fit it all together really help you and me? Will it help us better understand who we are, what the future holds, how we can better live here and now? Will it really help us in our personal relationships, in our marriages and families, in our jobs? Can it give us more than just advice on how to handle crises? the death of a loved one? the financial fallout of losing a job? catastrophic illness? betrayal by a friend? the seduction of our values? the abuses of the heart and soul? Will it allay our fears and calm our restlessness and heal our wounds? Can it really get us in touch with the same power that gave birth to the universe? that parted the Red Sea? that raised Jesus from the stranglehold of the grave? Can we really find unconditional love, total forgiveness, and genuine healing in its pages?

Yes. Yes. Without a shred of doubt.

The *Spirit-Filled Life Bible Discovery Guide* series is designed to help you unwrap, assemble, and enjoy all God has for you in the pages of Scripture. It will focus your time and energy on the books of the Bible, the people and places they describe, and the themes and life applications that flow thick from its pages like honey oozing from a beehive.

So you can get the most out of God's Word, this series has a number of helpful features. Each study guide has no more than fourteen lessons, each arranged so you can plumb the depths or skim the surface, depending on your needs and interests.

The study guides also contain six major sections, each marked by a symbol and heading for easy identification.

WORD WEALTH

The WORD WEALTH feature provides important definitions of key terms.

BEHIND THE SCENES

BEHIND THE SCENES supplies information about cultural beliefs and practices, doctrinal disputes, business trades, and the like, that illuminate Bible passages and teachings.

AT A GLANCE

The AT A GLANCE feature uses maps and charts to identify places and simplify themes or positions.

BIBLE EXTRA

Because this study guide focuses on a book of the Bible, you will find a BIBLE EXTRA feature that guides you into Bible dictionaries, Bible encyclopedias, and other resources that will enable you to glean more from the Bible's wealth if you want something extra.

PROBING THE DEPTHS

Another feature, PROBING THE DEPTHS, will explain controversial issues raised by particular lessons and cite Bible passages and other sources to which you can turn to help you come to your own conclusions.

FAITH ALIVE

Finally, each lesson contains a FAITH ALIVE feature. Here the focus is, So what? Given what the Bible says, what does it mean for my life? How can it impact my day-to-day needs, hurts, relationships, concerns, and whatever else is important to me? FAITH ALIVE will help you see and apply the practical relevance of God's literary gift.

As you'll see, these guides supply space for you to answer the study and life-application questions and exercises. You may, however, want to record all your answers, or just the overflow from your study or application, in a separate notebook or journal. This would be especially helpful if you think you'll dig into the BIBLE EXTRA features. Because the exercises in this feature are optional and can be expanded as far as you want to take them, we have not allowed writing space for them in this study guide. So you may want to have a notebook or journal handy for recording your discoveries while working through to this feature's riches.

The Bible study method used in this series revolves around four basic steps: observation, interpretation, correlation, and application. Observation answers the question, What does the text say? Interpretation deals with, What does the text mean?—not with what it means to you or me, but what it meant to its original readers. Correlation asks, What light do other Scripture passages shed on this text? And application, the goal of Bible study, poses the question, How should my life change in response to the Holy Spirit's teaching of this text?

If you have used a Bible much before, you know that it comes in a variety of translations and paraphrases. Although you can use any of them with profit as you work through the *Spirit-Filled Life Bible Discovery Guide* series, when Bible passages or words are cited, you will find they are from the New King James Version of the Bible. Using this translation with this series will make your study easier, but it's certainly not necessary.

The only resources you need to complete and apply these study guides are a heart and mind open to the Holy Spirit, a prayerful attitude, and a pencil and a Bible. Of course, you may draw upon other sources, such as commentaries, dictionaries, encyclopedias, atlases, and concordances, and you'll even find some optional exercises that will guide you into these sources. But these are extras, not necessities. These study guides are comprehensive enough to give you all you need to gain a good, basic understanding of the Bible book being covered and how you can apply its themes and counsel to your life.

A word of warning, though. By itself, Bible study will not transform your life. It will not give you power, peace, joy, comfort, hope, and a number of other gifts God longs for you to unwrap and enjoy. Through Bible study, you will grow in your understanding of the Lord, His kingdom and your place in it, and those things are essential. But you need more. You need to rely on the Holy Spirit to guide your study and your application of the Bible's truths. He, Jesus promised, was sent to teach us "all things" (John 14:26; cf. 1 Cor. 2:13). So as you use this series to guide you through Scripture, bathe your study time in prayer, asking the Spirit of God to illuminate the text, enlighten your mind, humble your will, and comfort your heart. He will never let you down.

My prayer and goal for you is that as you unwrap and begin to explore God's Book for living His way, the Holy Spirit will fill every fiber of your being with the joy and power God longs to give all His children. So read on. Be diligent. Stay open and submissive to Him. You will not be disappointed. He promises you!

INTRODUCTION

". . . the rude, the crude, and the lewd!"

The radio preacher's terminology was startling. He was describing the content of many modern films and forms of entertainment. He stressed how today's movies, TV programs, music videos, and records are negatively impacting children, families, and the moral fabric of this country.

"By the time the average youth reaches age sixteen," the preacher said, "he or she will have seen more than 200,000 acts of violence and 33,000 murders. Movies are reviewed and rated by the degree of socially offensive language, excessive violence, and/or graphic nudity. TV 'soap operas'—both in the daytime and evening prime time—are admittedly seeing 'just how far we can push it.' "

The radio preacher repeated his startling comment: "We are living in a land of the rude, the crude, and the lewd!"

THE CORINTHIAN CONTEXT

On the threshold of the third millennium since the birth of the Christian church, modern society is not unlike the sensual society and pagan culture the apostle Paul found in ancient Corinth. The practical need for spiritual purity and power to overcome "the world, the flesh, and the devil" is equally evident then and now. As a wealthy commercial center and port city on the southern tip of Greece, Corinth was known for its great temple of Aphrodite (the Greek goddess of love), with its 1,000 ritual priestess-prostitutes. The immoral conditions of Corinth are vividly seen in the fact that the Greek term *Korinthiazomai* (literally, "to act the Corinthian") came to mean "to practice fornication." Corinth was noted for its carnality.

In that setting, the apostle Paul had planted a church during his second missionary journey (Acts 18:1–17). What were the names of the husband-and-wife team he met in Corinth? (v. 2)

Why did he stay with them? (v. 3)

What was the theme of his message to the Jews? (v. 5)

Was his witness successful in the synagogue? Why? (v. 6)

What significant new strategy did Paul announce to the Jews? (v. 6)

THE CORINTHIAN CORRESPONDENCE

It was probably about five years later, approximately A.D. 55, during Paul's three-year ministry in Ephesus on his third missionary journey, that he wrote the epistle known today as 1 Corinthians. In it Paul responded to disturbing reports and questions about life in this problematic congregation. He had received reports of sectarian divisions and moral disorders within the church. Additionally, a delegation had arrived from Corinth, and (or with) a letter seeking his advice on various difficulties and critical issues in the spiritually gifted but morally weak congregation.

This first correspondence consists of Paul's response to problems related to ten separate issues: a sectarian spirit, incest, lawsuits, fornication, marriage and divorce, eating food offered to idols, wearing of the veil, the Lord's Supper, spiritual gifts, and the resurrection of the human body. With each problem Paul pointed to spiritual solutions. He wanted the Corinthians to learn new "pathways to pure power."

The second epistle of Paul to this same congregation (excluding a now lost letter he alludes to in 1 Corinthians 5:9 and 2 Corinthians 2:4; 7:6–8) is more autobiographical and pastoral. In it Paul presents his personal character in defense of his ministry and his God-given authority as an apostle. This study guide will focus on the first epistle only.

CONTEMPORARY CONCLUSIONS

Corinth was a first-century church with many problems: sectarianism, spiritual immaturity, church discipline, immoral practices, the roles of the sexes, and the proper use of spiritual gifts. Where these same problems exist in the modern church, the remedies are the same. Studying the godly guidelines and applying the practical "pathways to pure power" revealed in this epistle will establish devoted disciples and heal the problems of contemporary churches that may exist—as Corinth—in a ". . . land of the rude, the crude, and the lewd."

PROBING THE DEPTHS

Further study in certain commentaries and other resources will help prepare you for the instruction and insight into practical Christian belief and behavior which Paul gives to the Corinthians in this epistle. Some helpful general resources include:

> *Nelson's Illustrated Bible Dictionary,* Herbert Lockyer, Sr., General Editor, Thomas Nelson Publishers.
> *Spirit-Filled Life Bible,* Jack W. Hayford, General Editor, Thomas Nelson Publishers.
> *The Word Bible Handbook,* Lawrence O. Richards, Word Books.
> *The Communicator's Commentary,* 1, 2 Corinthians, Kenneth L. Chafin, Word Books.

With these (or other) reference resources, probe the depths of the thoughts and terms of Paul's introduction in his first epistle to the Corinthians (1:1–9):

How did Paul describe himself at the beginning of both Corinthian letters? (1:1)

Was this common in Paul's correspondence? (Check the opening verses of some of Paul's other epistles.) Why?

Look up the word *apostle* in a Bible dictionary. Give its primary meaning in both the Old and New Testaments:

Paul's claim of apostolic authority was based on two significant factors. Review the following scriptures and then list those factors: (Acts 9:1–6, 15; 26:15–18; 1 Cor. 15:3–8; 1 Tim. 2:7).

How did Peter classify Paul's writings? (2 Pet. 3:14–16)

How did that validate Paul's claim of apostolic authority?

What kind of people were in the church at Corinth? (1:2)

How did Paul describe them in his greeting? (1:2, 3)

Consult a Bible dictionary and then define the words "sanctified" and "saints."

Does Paul's use of the term "saint" imply perfection or potential? (Rom. 1:17; 2 Thess. 1:10–12 and Jude 3.)

What qualities and characteristics of life should be seen in people who are "sanctified saints"? (Rom. 12:1, 2; 1 Thess. 4:1–8.)

What did Paul thank God for in the lives and experiences of the Corinthian believers? (1:4)

In what ways had they been "enriched?" (1:5–7)

Paul's confidence that they would be declared "blameless" in the day of our Lord Jesus Christ" was based on what? (1:8, 9)

FAITH ALIVE

As you conclude this introduction to Paul's "pathways to pure power," explain how God gives His children mercy and not justice.

Share how His mercy directly affected you recently.

Have there been times when you have been spiritually fickle and not faithful? When was the last time?

Now, thank God that He is faithful and will "confirm [guarantee] you to the end" (1:8)! And thank His Son, Jesus Christ, our Lord, for His fellowship, grace, and peace. Write your prayer of praise here:

Lesson 1/Rival Cliques
(1:10—4:21)

Two youngsters were playing. One turned to the other and asked innocently, "What abomination do you belong to?"

Religious denominations have evolved within the larger body of Christ in recent centuries. But distinct groups of dissenting believers also surfaced in the first decades of the early church. As the gospel spread from "Jerusalem . . . Judea . . . Samaria, and to the end of the earth" (Acts 1:8), the fellowship of believers was often interrupted by human separations based on ethnic, geographical, sociological, and doctrinal distinctives.

Paul told the Galatians that when Peter (Cephas) arrived at Antioch, he (Paul) had "withstood him to his face." Why? (Gal. 2:11–21)

If God morally justifies all sinners because of their faith in Jesus and not because of any works of the Law (Gal. 2:16), is there ever justification for discrimination or separation among believers? Why or why not?

CORINTHIAN CLIQUES
(1:10–17)

The first problem Paul addressed in his first letter to the Corinthians was the foolishness of factionalism. A major sectarian spirit had developed in their circles of fellowship over quarrels about their favorite preachers. All of this was based on their supposed superior wisdom. These divisions had shattered the unity of the local congregation and created dissension.

Paul began by tenderly exhorting them and pleading with them (1:10). The Greek word translated here as "plead," *parakaleo*, means "to call alongside." The idea conveys an active work of encouraging and helping someone get back on the right track.

He urged the Corinthian Christians to have "no divisions among [them]" (1:10). *Divisions* comes from the word *schisma*, meaning "to separate, to rip, to tear, to split." This body of believers Paul had loved and nurtured to life is now broken and divided over many issues:

Preachers (1:12)

Immorality (5:1, 2)

Going to Law Before the Heathen (6:1–11)

Marriage (7:1–40)

Meats Offered to Idols (8:1–13)

Conduct of Women in the Church (11:1–16)

The Lord's Table (11:17–34)

Spiritual Gifts (12:1—14:40)

The Resurrection (15:1–58)

Unity is vitally important to any church or fellowship. Paul did not mean all Christians must agree on everything, but that there should be unity of spirit and purpose. The word translated "perfectly joined together" is also used of the "mending" of the disciples' nets in the Gospels (Matt. 4:21). Torn nets won't catch fish; they must be mended. Neither can a church torn by internal dissension win men and women to Christ or enjoy the flow of God's grace and power.

FAITH ALIVE

In your opinion, what kind of issues threaten unity in the body of Christ today? (List at least three.)

Do you see them as essential or peripheral issues? Why?

Do you think of them as temporal or eternal issues? Explain.

BEHIND THE SCENES

This Corinthian congregation met in houses or halls. It is easy to see how separations (or sects) could develop based on natural loyalties to gifted leaders and comparisons among certain styles of ministry and services (1:10–12). All of these men had strong personalities, developed spiritual gifts, and well-honed natural abilities. All of these traits were energized by God for His holy purposes. If society at large can be classified as either leaders or followers, these were leaders. But the ongoing contentions among the young believers contaminated their fellowship and their witness. Diversity is of God (1 Cor. 12:4–7); division is of the Devil (Prov. 6:16–19).

Paul confronted them about their quarrels and their cliques. There seemed to be three main groups. Some were identifying with their founding pastor; others with the eloquent teacher who came to Corinth after the founder left for Jerusalem; still others identified with one of the closest of Jesus' disciples. A fourth sect, in their pride, claimed exclusive rights to the label "Christian" (1:12). This latter group may have been a particularly pious party who refused to recognize the authority of any human minister. Still others were boasting about who had baptized them (1:13). It is not clear if this was just a boast or if they had come to rest the authenticity of their faith on the human baptizer.

The Corinthians needed to learn that they were "all baptized into one body" by the Spirit of God (12:13). Whoever baptized a believer in water was unimportant. The Corinthians had missed the point regarding Paul's teaching concerning water baptism. Paul was emphasizing that the central thrust of the gospel had to do with faith in Jesus Christ and that no one should have inordinate allegiance to any man just because they were baptized by that man.

What a shame to limit God by supposing that only one preacher or church or style of ministry can be used of God to bless or build His people. Can you think of any arrogant attitudes like that in religious circles today? If so, identify and describe the situation(s).

 FAITH ALIVE

Do you feel Paul's remarks in 1 Corinthians 1:14–17 minimize the doctrine of water baptism? Why or why not?

Was water baptism practiced during Paul's pastorate in Corinth? Use Acts 18:8 and 1 Corinthians 1:14–17 to explain your answer.

Why do you think Paul's call was to "preach the gospel," and why did he say, "For Christ did not send me to baptize"?

Did Jesus actually baptize His disciples? (John 4:1ff.)

BEHIND THE SCENES

Those who rallied around the name of Paul were probably Gentiles who gloried in the great principles of liberty preached by Paul as he showed how the gospel displaced the Jewish law. However, they may have been "pushing" their liberties to an extreme and becoming a hindrance rather than a help to the acceptance of the gospel of Christ.

Apollos (1:12) was a Jewish Christian from Alexandria, the famed city of learning on the Mediterranean coast of Egypt. It was there the Septuagint, the Jewish translation of the Hebrew Scriptures into Greek (used by Jesus and the early church) was prepared. When Apollos arrived in Ephesus, Aquila and Priscilla took him home for fuller instruction (Acts 18:24ff.). He later traveled to the province of Achaia (of which Corinth was the capital), where he proved a powerful and eloquent teacher and "greatly helped those who had believed through grace; for he vigorously refuted the Jews publicly, showing from the Scriptures that Jesus is the Christ" (Acts 18:27b, 28).

It is not clear whether the mention of Peter (Cephas, 1:12) means he visited and ministered in Corinth. There is no record of this in Acts. However, since he was a leader of the twelve apostles, it would be natural for a personality cult to form around his name, particularly among the Jewish believers.

What is clear, however, is that the rival cliques were making comparisons between Paul and the more eloquent Apollos. Paul, although a trained scholar, had had his problems at Corinth (Acts 18:9, 10; 1 Cor. 2:3). Having failed to make spiritual headway among the "heady" philosophers of Athens, Paul seemed to change his approach when he arrived in Corinth. Profound simplicity of speech and power manifestations were more important to him than polished oration (2:3–5).

THE REPROACH OF THE GOSPEL
(1:18—2:16)

Perhaps the Corinthians were influenced by the culture of nearby Athens. They seemed to fancy themselves as thinkers and took pride in their supposed intellectual superiority. Paul reminded them that human cleverness is not necessarily God's way or wisdom (1:18—2:16). God's plan of salvation through Christ's death on the Cross is often rejected by wise and clever people. Those who are spiritually wise perceive truth by the Spirit and not the mind alone. This kind of wisdom is God's gift through His Holy Spirit.

Proud and clever people are not the ones who appreciate the wisdom of God's plan of salvation through Christ's death on the Cross, but those who are spiritually wise. According to 1 Corinthians 3:18, one must actually become a "fool" in the world's eyes in order to be really wise.

One does not have to "check his brains at the door" when he becomes a Christian. Human wisdom has its place. God has equipped us with wondrous knowledge, giving us dominion over the earth and intelligence to travel to the moon and back. The capacity of the human mind is beyond comprehension.

Paul's attack on human wisdom (1 Cor. 1:18–31) does not belittle the gift of human intelligence. But the answer to humankind's dilemma is not intellectual and cultural; it is moral and spiritual. The cure is the Cross of Christ—not merely the wooden instrument of death, but the sacrifice that took place there—and the subsequent resurrection of our Lord, His ascension, and finally the bestowal of His Spirit on all those who believe.

But God's "holy foolishness" is at odds with humankind's "wise" ways. Neither the Jews' "do a miracle" approach, nor the Gentiles' philosophical approach (1:22) can grasp the power and wisdom God expressed in the Cross. It is an issue of false versus true wisdom.

Paul further points out the inferior intellectual and social status of many of the believers. He explained: "God has chosen the foolish things of the world to put to shame the wise, and God has chosen the weak things of the world to put to shame the things which are mighty" (1:27).

But the results are powerful and eternal. Each believer is "in Christ," and He provides "righteousness and sanctification and redemption" (1:30). Therefore, "he who glories, let him glory in the Lord" (v. 31).

This "holy foolishness" is illustrated further by Paul's plain manner of preaching and in the convincing power of the Spirit (2:1–5). The purpose was that the faith of the believing

Corinthians would not be in man's cleverness, but in the power of God (2:5).

However, true wisdom is revealed by the Spirit (2:6–13) to those who are "mature." This maturity is like a fruit which has developed to completion and perfection; it is ripe.

BIBLE EXTRA

Spiritual maturity involves many things. Hebrews 5:11–14 teaches three principles about spiritual maturity as compared with spiritual immaturity:

First, *maturity takes time* (v. 12). The believers need to be exposed to the truth of the Word and see it modeled in others over a period of time. God will apply it to the individual life.

Second, *maturity involves growth in the knowledge of the Word of God* (v. 13). Babies in Christ are able only to handle the simple things of the gospel (1 Pet. 2:2). Spiritual development (or deformity) is directly related to the amount of intake of the Word.

Finally, *spiritual maturity involves experience in the use of the Word in discerning between good and bad, or truth and error* (vv. 13, 14). This is to be a disciplined exercise in spiritual discernment.

CARNALITY IS THE CAUSE
(3:1–4)

This sectarian spirit was evidence to the apostle Paul that some of the spiritually gifted believers in the Corinthian church were actually "carnal . . . behaving like *mere* men" (3:3, 4). When there exists carnal behavior (such as "envy, strife, and divisions"), carnality (relying on the basic nature of the weak, sinful, human flesh) must be the cause.

It is often expressed in a weak and frustrated Christian accompanied by a poor prayer life, not studying the Bible, and limited Christian fellowship. A carnal life-style increases our vulnerability to temptation and sin.

FAITH ALIVE

True Spiritual Growth Requires God's Word (3:1–5). Beginning in 1 Corinthians 2:10, Paul elaborates our need of Holy Spirit-given wisdom and revelation, and he ties this very firmly to our receiving the "words" which the Holy Spirit teaches" (2:13). He immediately turns from these observations to an outright confrontation with the carnality of the Corinthians, attributing it to the shallowness of their intake of God's Word ("not able to receive [solid food]," 3:2; see also Heb. 5:12–15).

The demanding truth of this passage is that no amount of supposed spiritual insight or experience reflects genuine spiritual growth if it is separated from our basic growth in the knowledge of God's Word in the Bible. Without this rootedness in the Word, we may be deluded about our growth. Such "rootedness" is in truth and love, not merely in learning knowledge or accomplished study. In order to experience true spiritual growth, we must spend time in the Word and separate ourselves from the hindrances of lovelessness, competitiveness, and strife.[1]

BIBLE EXTRA

The solution to carnality is developed throughout the New Testament. According to the Apostle Paul, a first step is to *appropriate the power of the Holy Spirit* and no longer "walk according to the flesh, but according to the Spirit" (Rom. 8:1).

Give three reasons why those who are "in Christ" are no longer obligated to serve sin? (Rom. 8:1–14)

1.

2.

3.

Partners in Ministry
(3:5–17)

Paul goes on to try to explain that he and Apollos are not rivals but partners, sharing the work of building God's church (3:5–9). Using the imagery of a garden, he said that one minister plants, another waters the seed, another reaps—but it is God who produces the life. Therefore, the human instrument is inconsequential.

He then changed the imagery to that of a building (3:9) and called himself "a wise master builder" who laid the foundation, which is Jesus Christ (v. 11). Other men have been building upon what he started. Their work, in the sense of their teaching, was of three types: (1) some employed enduring materials such as "gold, silver, precious stones"—the wisdom of the gospel, which is divinely revealed truth; (2) others built with flammable materials such as "wood, hay, straw" (or sticks, grass and straw)—perhaps more human wisdom or worldly church practices; and (3) some tended to destroy God's temple by causing division within the local congregation.

The passage has both a pastoral and an ongoing personal application. Once the basic foundation of faith in Christ is laid, every Christian is responsible for what he does with the new life he has been given. We must see to it that we build to last (3:10–17).

The issue in Scripture seems to be twofold: what are we building with our lives (and churches) today, and what materials are we using? It is clear that some believers may have their life's service judged as worthless and receive no reward other than the assurance of heaven itself (vv. 15, 16).

 Faith Alive

What building materials are described in verse 12?

What do you think they represent in a believer's life?

How do they relate to each other?

What will the fire test or reveal? (v. 13)

What will determine if an individual will receive a reward? (vv. 13, 14)

How should the fact that God's Spirit lives in every Christian affect the way we live? (v. 16)

In what ways have you been able to plant and water God's Word in others this week?

What could you do in your church this month to help build up other Christians?

SPIRITUAL LEADERSHIP
(4:1–21)

Paul goes on in 1 Corinthians 4 to provide some background for helping the local groups within the Corinthian congregation learn how to judge and evaluate their leaders.

FAITH ALIVE

How are we to treat persons who are in a position of ministry leadership?

Are we to look up to them? Respect them higher than others? Why or why not?

Give them any special powers or privileges? Why or why not?

How can congregations show honor without putting pastors on a pedestal?

First, Paul reminds them of a leader's responsibility as a steward and as an example (vv. 1–5). From a personal perspective, a leader or Christian worker is a representative of Jesus Christ. His conversion, his call, his gifts are from above. Wise believers will respect God's servant, not because of his pulpit oratory, his sparkling personality, or his administrative genius, but because he is the Lord's representative. And wiser still is the pastor or Christian worker who remembers with deep humility that he represents the Lord, not because of any wonderful qualities in himself, but because the Lord has allowed him such a holy calling. As one pastor put it, "God wrote the message, and I am just the messenger boy."

In a sense, each believer is a "steward" (4:1). This word in Greek, *oikonomos,* comes from two words meaning "house" and "to arrange." The word originally referred to the manager of a household or estate, and then in a broader sense denoted an administrator or a steward in general.

All believers are stewards (1 Pet. 4:10), but in a particular way this is true of a spiritual leader. The Master, in His absence, has made him an overseer of His work. The Christian worker is a servant of Christ and a steward "of the mysteries of God" (1 Cor. 4:1). "Mysteries" here are not literary "whodunits," but God's great plan of redemption, which was originally unknown to mankind, but now made crystal clear by the writings and teachings of the apostles and prophets. The minister (or "servant") is held accountable both to know and to faithfully give out these great truths of God's Word as he would preach "the whole counsel of God" (Acts 20:27).

From a public perspective, Paul offered himself as an example (1 Cor. 4:3, 4). He felt he had a clear conscience before any human court of evaluation, but acknowledged his final judgment was with God, who alone is fully competent to offer perfect judgment. Human evaluations meant little to the apostle. Such judgments are frequently faulty, shallow, and premature. Too often they are mere criticism based on personal preferences and not facts or Scripture.

Only divine judgment is perfect, and that time of judgment is coming. The only proper time for complete evaluation of a Christian worker's merit is still future—"until the Lord comes" (4:5).

Second, Paul challenged them about a leader's relationship with his sheep. Just as the spiritual maturity and the fruitful service of a church depend much on a leader's qualifications, so is there much dependence on the quality of those being led. A good relationship between the two is necessary. When mutual trust, love, and respect are lost, Christ's cause is seriously damaged.

Paul demonstrated a "servant-leader" style that was very transparent and "incarnational." He first lived out the basic truths in his own life and then explained and taught them to those he led. He opened the pages of Scripture and also the doors of his own heart so that others not only heard the truth but saw the process by which it was believed and incorporated into a life of faith.

FAITH ALIVE

Though the Corinthians were "puffed up" with pride (4:6, 18, 19), Paul sought to humble them without rejecting them. He first appealed to reason (vv. 6, 7) and used his pen as a rod to correct the wayward saints.

Apparently there was a strong streak of spiritual arrogance among these early believers. Drawn into unwise and unhealthy exaltation of human leadership, they seemed to feel they had a "corner on the truth." They looked down their noses with contempt at other believers not marching to their own personal drumbeat.

Paul corrected the Corinthians with three rhetorical questions, which hurt their egos (v. 7).

1. "Who makes you differ *from another*?" Were they really superior to any other believer or group?

2. "What do you have that you did not receive?" Who gave them the gospel? Who gave them salvation? Who gave them milk and solid food for spiritual growth?

3. "Why do you boast as if you had not received *it*?"

Their silent response to these questions spoke volumes.

Like the Corinthians, our abilities and blessings come from God; we cannot take credit for them. They are God's gifts, and our use of them is our gift to God. They are to be used in service and blessing to others and not selfishly kept for our exclusive enjoyment.

A TENDER REBUKE
(4:8–13)

Paul then resorted to a kind of sanctified sarcasm (vv. 8–13) as he delivered a needed rebuke. The Corinthian church, somewhere near the fifth anniversary of their founding, felt they had reached the pinnacle of spiritual attainment. In prideful conceit, the believers regarded themselves as now possessing more "revelation" and spiritual attainment than their founder and teachers. Paul longed for the day when the Corinthian church would evidence all the spiritual maturity they thought they already possessed.

Paul's paternal care is shown in the final verses of this tender rebuke. Because he had founded the church, he had a special fatherly role in the life of its people. Though they had had many "instructors in Christ," he alone had been their spiritual father. In his attempt to unify the church, he appealed to this important role and relationship. As he transitioned to a tough conclusion in which he spoke very directly about their sin, he wanted them to know his words were motivated by love—like a good father has for his children (1 Thess. 2:11).

 ### FAITH ALIVE

Who has been a "father in the faith" to you?

What are the characteristics of this kind of person?

Have you told them "thank you" recently? When? How?

Who would consider *you* a "spiritual parent"? Why?

Paul based his "tough-love" conclusion on the strength of a leader's reasonable authority of position and example. Paul consistently presented a well-balanced, disciplined, and godly life-style. He did not desire his converts to become attached to him personally. Rather, he wanted them to imitate him in attitude, faithfulness, and singleness of purpose; thus, they would become imitators of Christ.

Paul told them he was sending Timothy to them, whom he described as "my beloved and faithful son in the Lord" (4:17). Timothy was familiar to the congregation in that he traveled with Paul on his second missionary journey (see Acts

16:1–3). Following a modern management precept ("people do what you *inspect*, not necessarily what you *expect*") Timothy was to see that Paul's advice was received, read, and implemented. He was then to return to Paul and report on the church's progress.

Later, Paul planned to visit the Corinthians personally, if the Lord permitted (vv. 18–21). If his correction was received, if the cliques were broken, if unity was restored, he could greet them with love. Otherwise, he would bring severe rebuke. The choice was theirs.

1. *Spirit-Filled Life Bible* (Nashville, TN: Thomas Nelson Publishers, 1991), 1722, "Kingdom Dynamics: True Spiritual Growth Requires God's Word."

Lesson 2/Moral Failures
(5:1–13)

The term "dysfunctional family" is one currently heard in pop psychology. It can describe anything from loud, abusive arguments to emotional, physical, or even sexual abuse by family members.

The Corinthian church could be called a "dysfunctional family" in the spiritual sense. They manifested moral failure, which impacted each member as well as their witness to the world around them. First, they tolerated an outrageous case of incest, and then tried to excuse it in the name of supposed spiritual maturity. In addition, their common witness was stained on the witness stand of civil courts as they joined the litigation mania of the secular society and brought lawsuits against other believers. Finally, the Corinthians, ignoring the sanctity of the human body, had allowed perverted practices of the world to taint their moral standards.

Paul's corrective letter to the Corinthians bluntly charged that their behavior contradicted their beliefs. He seemed as much concerned about the arrogant attitude of the church toward these flagrant sins as he did about the sins themselves. Their "puffed up" pride (5:2) kept them from having a godly grief about such offenses to God and humankind. They seemed to deny the reality of the wrongs, wanting instead merely to go on with their religion.

IMMORALITY DEFILES THE CHURCH
(5:1–8)

Church history and modern tabloids are full of examples of church leaders and laymen who, instead of becoming in action what they profess to believe, presumptuously seek to justify their ungodly behavior. Their presumed "maturity" is supposed to license clear violations of the Word.

Make several observations from 1 Corinthians 5:1, 2 about the gross immorality that had invaded the church at Corinth.

How secret was the scandal?

What exactly was the sin?

What was the reaction of the godless Gentiles in the community?

How would their behavior have looked if it had matched their beliefs? (v. 2)

Paul does not make a case for believers to pry into the personal lives of other believers. It is unwholesome and unChristian for church leadership to attempt to be detectives, prosecutors, and judges over every area of life for its members. The brotherhood of believers is to be built upon mutual affection and confidence, not doubt and suspicion. God is able to make the secret things come to light without vigilante groups following each other home to see if there is something amiss behind the curtains.

However, when sin has become public knowledge it must be confronted lest it infect the whole body. A good principle is that the correction should extend to the degree the sin has extended (Matt. 18:15–17). If the sin is confessed while it is yet private and not public, then the corrective steps should be kept private. However, if the sin is public knowledge, then the correction needs to be public as well (1 Tim. 5:20).

The expression "his father's wife" (5:1) is thought to mean a stepmother. It is the same expression as in Leviticus 18:8 and Deuteronomy 22:30, where marriage to close relatives is forbidden in the Law of Moses. Israelites who violated these laws could be executed. It is certain it was not the offender's mother, but the wife of his father. Either she is his father's widow, or perhaps the woman is divorced from his father.

Usually God's standards are in stark contrast to the social standards of those in the regular society among whom God's people must live. Their beliefs and behavior make them stand out as a "peculiar" or set apart as "sanctified" people. But here, the apathetic attitude of the Corinthian believers was even repulsive to the pagans. This practice of incest was even prohibited by Roman law. Though there are accounts of Roman emperors marrying whomever they pleased, this open incest was an affront to the general public.

 FAITH ALIVE

Why do you think the Corinthian congregation tolerated this immorality in their community?

How did Paul suggest they should have responded? (v. 2)

How do you view blatant sin among believers? Like the Corinthians, do you shrug it off? Why?

How does God see it? (Ps. 78:40; Jer. 23:9, 10; Ezek. 6:9)

Like Joshua and Caleb of the Old Testament (Num. 13:30; 14:6–9), Paul took a stand against the majority opinion in the Corinthian congregation when he said: "For I indeed, as absent in body but present in spirit, have already judged (as though I were present) him who has so done this deed" (5:3). Paul criticized their prideful permissiveness, which allowed professed believers to more or less do whatever they wanted to, even if it violated clear commands of Scripture. This is a perverted view of God's grace.

In the rest of chapter 5, Paul gives the Corinthians clear instruction on how to handle the scandal in a disciplined, but redemptive manner. The principles learned here are based on the Bible's teaching to discern between good and evil and the necessity for believers to behave accordingly.

 FAITH ALIVE

What special circumstances were to accompany the expulsion of the immoral member? (5:4, 5) Why?

Why was it necessary for the Corinthian church to expel the man from their congregation?

Do you find it easy to be full of indignation at sin and yet full of compassion for the sinner?

Is it loving or cruel to allow our brothers and sisters to be broad-minded and permit sin to reign in their lives? Why?

Do you have friends or family members who need to discern right from wrong before such a drastic discipline would need to be taken in their lives? Explain.

BEHIND THE SCENES

Paul instructed the Corinthian church to assemble and publicly hand the guilty person over to Satan "for the destruction of the flesh, that his spirit may be saved in the day of the Lord Jesus" (5:5). How are we to understand such drastic terms? What insight do the following scriptures give to the phrase, "deliver such a one to Satan"?

1 Tim. 1:20

Titus 3:10, 11

Some have suggested that the "destruction of the flesh" meant sickness or even premature death under the chastening hand of God. What can you learn from the following scriptures?

1 Cor. 11:27–32

1 John 5:16

The assembled church meant that the discipline would be graciously administered corporately by the elders, who had responsibility for spiritual oversight, and not by individual members.

These divine directives require church leadership to judge those things that God has declared in His Word to be sin. He has already spoken, and the actions of the leaders are in agreement with His in the spirit realm and are to be confirmed in the natural realm by the united disapproval of all the assembled believers. This was to be done "in the name of our Lord Jesus," with the spiritually mature leaders acting as the agents of our Lord. This serious and solemn action was to be carried out as though Jesus Christ Himself were administering it with all His authority and power (1 Cor 5:4).

Paul called for this corrective action not as punishment, but as a necessary step toward restoration and ultimate victory. Without discipline, we are not disciples. Discipline brings not only correction to the erring brother or sister, but also protection for the testimony of the local body of believers.

BIBLE EXTRA

The various problems and issues that arise in personal relationships and Christian fellowship may call for various levels of correction and discipline in Scripture: personal differences, doctrinal error, overt sin, gross immorality, a failing elder, and more. The Bible gives insightful guidelines to follow in faithfully discharging the church's duty to lovingly correct and discipline in these cases. Often such action is the responsibility of the "shepherds" and "overseers" of the congregation, "for they watch out for your souls, as those who must give account" (Heb. 13:17).

However, affirmative action is also incumbent on each believer (2 John 10, 11). Sometimes we must rebuke a brother, whereas the same type of behavior displayed by a non-Christian should be accepted graciously on behalf of Christ, who was called a "friend of . . . sinners" (Matt. 11:19).

What principles concerning church discipline can you find in the following scriptures?

Matt. 18:15–18

2 Thess. 3:6–15

1 Tim. 5:17–21

1 Tim. 6:3–5

2 Tim. 2:24–26

Titus 3:9–11

Heb. 12:11

James 5:19, 20

Jude 22, 23

   Paul did not explain exactly how they were to "deliver" the unrepenting party to Satan. It is clear that he was to be excluded from the public fellowship of the church as well as the private activities of the believers (1 Cor. 5:9–13). In fact, Paul commanded them "not even to eat with such a person" (v. 11). In practice, this may be extremely difficult when family relations, neighbors, or business associations are involved. However, the obedient believer has a solemn responsibility to see that the judgment pronounced by the leadership "in the name of our Lord Jesus Christ" is carried out for the good of all involved.

   In addition to physical and social separation, this was to be a physical action illustrating a spiritual reality. Jesus taught there is a heavenly recognition and ratification of earthly trans-actions when they are handled according to divine directions

(Matt. 18:18). This may be how they "loosed" the guilty party (Matt. 18:17–20) to the consequences of his repeated and unrepented sins.

Rare is the church that endeavors to lovingly and fully follow the biblical commands in this sensitive area.

FAITH ALIVE

Why is church discipline so infrequently practiced in congregations today?

Is this true in your church? Why?

Is it possible one of the reasons for the lack of spiritual power in many contemporary churches is failure to follow this biblical principle of corporate discipline? Explain.

As it was the custom of Jews before the Passover to cleanse their homes from all leaven, so the church is here admonished to clean out the immoral practices from its midst (5:7). Leaven (yeast), as used in Scripture as a type of sin, spreads through the whole batch of dough. Blatant sin which is condoned, overlooked, rationalized, or unjudged likewise will spread and confuse and divide the whole church. Therefore, it must be purged out.

The reason? Jesus Christ, the Passover Lamb, who takes away the sin of the world (Ex. 12:1–13; John 1:29), has been offered. It is faith in His shed blood and substitutionary death on the Cross that is our only hope of salvation. The Old Testament Feast of Unleavened Bread, which the Paschal sacrifice inaugurated (Ex. 12:12–22), is a "type" of the Christian life being lived in separation from sin and in sincerity and truth (1 Cor. 5:8).

WORD WEALTH

Sincerity, *eilikrineia.* Literally, "judged by sunlight." The word alludes to Oriental bazaars where pottery was displayed in dimly lit rooms. Unscrupulous merchants would patch cracked pottery or cover defects with wax. Intelligent buyers would hold up the pottery to the sun and judge its quality by the sunlight. *Eilikrineia* is a transparent honesty, genuine purity, manifested clarity, and unsullied innocence. It describes one who does not fear thorough examination of his motives and intents, because he has nothing to hide.[1]

IMMORALITY MUST BE JUDGED
(5:9–13)

Paul makes a clear and important distinction between sinners in the world and those in the church. The church leadership is to administer corrective discipline to those inside its fellowship, but judgment of those outside the church rests with God (5:12, 13). It is part of our witness to accept sinners in the world on their own terms. But it is foolhardy to condone clear violations of Scripture among the faithful.

Paul did not call for a monastic withdrawal from the worldly and sexually immoral people. Such practices have done little to advance godliness or the gospel. Instead, the things Paul mentioned as dividing lines for fellowship were things that Scripture also clearly identifies as sin elsewhere: idolatry, adultery, fornication, homosexuality, thievery, drunkenness. God has already announced His judgment on all of them (5:11; 6:9, 10). In these areas, the church must speak with God's voice. Our judgment must agree with His.

FAITH ALIVE

Is God's condemnation of these practices a judging of the sin or the sinner?

Is the individual to be disciplined by the fellowship for a single act or failure?

How have you prayed for any person who is a bad influence on you?

At what point would you stop associating with a professing believer who continued in gross sin?

To what extent should those who desire to become members of a local church body be living in moral and spiritual purity and be willing to submit to the demands of discipleship?

What is the difference regarding moral and spiritual accountability between a member of a local body or a supposedly mature Christian and a new convert who has just accepted Jesus Christ?

What deterrent value is church discipline to have in the body of Christ? (1 Tim. 5:20)

In summary, then, church discipline is to be employed when one who claims to be a member of the family of God is unrepentant and habitually practices something that the Word of God has unequivocally condemned as sin.

PROBING THE DEPTHS

Jesus' pattern for correction called for private reproof before public rejection (Matt. 18:15–17).

What if the sinning person sincerely repents? (2 Cor. 2:5–8)

What if there is no repentance? How should we respond in social contact with the disobedient person? (2 Thess. 3:14, 15)

What is the final action to be taken by church leadership to a sinning and unrepentant believer? (Titus 3:10)

Roy Knuteson's book, *Calling the Church to Discipline,* warns of failure in the attempt to discipline if there is not complete cooperation from the larger body of Christ in a given locality. "The proper way to handle such a matter is to do exactly what the Corinthians did. They barred him from their services and refused even to visit with him socially. He was confined to the sphere of the world instead of the church, for the object of this chastisement was the 'destruction of his flesh.' It must be remembered that in those days there was only one Christian assembly in this notoriously sinful Greek city, and there was no other spiritual fellowship and refreshment to be found anywhere. He could not, as in the case of many today, simply 'move his membership' elsewhere. There was no place to go. If churches today would communicate their actions to other churches, people could not run away from discipline measures in their local assemblies. When they do, the intended discipline fails and the church suffers."[2]

The final intent of the church discipline of the incestuous member in Corinth was "that his spirit may be saved" (1 Cor. 5:5). We are to discipline in order to restore, not destroy. Like

Father God, we love the sinning brother or sister; we hate their sin. Through discipline we invite our straying brother or sister to return to full fellowship with the Father and His family.

Genuine repentance prepares for restoration to God and to the local assembly. The first is immediate, the second cannot be. Proof of repentance is needed over a period of time, especially if the disciplined party had been in leadership in the local church. Healing and restoration of trust take time.

 BEHIND THE SCENES

In his book, *Restoring Fallen Leaders*, Jack Hayford has spoken with compassion and conviction regarding the need for sufficient attestation of genuine repentance:

"Sin isn't the fruit of a moment; neither is restoration.

"Although the basic worth of the individual's experience and wisdom has not been completely lost, and though he may well be 'sadder but wiser' for having failed, the fallen leader *must* reestablish a life-style verifying trustworthiness again. Time must be required to reestablish scriptural values in his conduct.

"The fruitage of: (1) orderly personal, church, and family relationships, (2) proper personal life and money management, and (3) reliability in living what is taught; all this must be given *time* to be verified.

"It is outright dishonesty with the psychological facts of the human personality to suppose an overnight or quick-fix healing in relationships or trust is as immediate as the blessing of God's instant forgiveness."[3]

Some believe that this man was restored to the church, because Paul wrote in his next letter: "But if anyone has caused grief, he has not grieved me, but all of you to some extent—not to be too severe. This punishment which *was inflicted* by the majority *is* sufficient for such a man, so that, on the contrary, you *ought* rather to forgive and comfort *him*, lest perhaps such a one be swallowed up with too much sorrow. Therefore I urge you to reaffirm *your* love for him" (2 Cor. 2:5–8).

1. *Spirit-Filled Life Bible* (Nashville, TN: Thomas Nelson Publishers, 1991), 1725, "Word Wealth: 5:8 sincerity."

2. Roy E. Knuteson, *Calling the Church to Discipline* (Nashville, TN: Action Press, 1977), 102.

3. Jack W. Hayford, *Restoring Fallen Leaders* (Ventura, CA: Regal Books, 1988), 38–40. Used by permission.

Lesson 3/The People's Court
(6:1–11)

The testimonies of the Corinthian believers were being stained on the witness stand of the People's Court! Rather than confine personal differences and contentions to the mediation of mature saints, they entered into public litigation. They failed to understand the biblical principle of separation.

As believers, we are "in the world," but not "of the world." Any perceived wrong among Christians is to be judged within the church (Matt. 18:15–17; 1 Cor. 5:12); God and the civil government He has instituted will judge those outside the church (1 Cor. 5:13). Paul had to exhort that it was wrong for those who were outside the church to be used to judge those on the inside (6:1). He went on to forcefully tell Corinthians that regardless of the outcome of the lawsuits, they were losers (v. 7)! They lost because of the failure of their Christian responsibility for brotherly love (Heb. 13:1). Now, because their behavior has not matched their beliefs, a brother or sister is publicly offended and the church is shamed.

When it comes to settling differences between believers, secular law courts do not compare with the community of faith. Christians at worship are in a place where confessions are made, forgiveness learned, and justice understood firsthand, with Christ Himself as the merciful Judge. Paul told the Philippians to follow the Lord's lead and consider the interests of others more important than their own (Phil. 2:1–8).

However, even among sincere and growing Christians there are differences of opinions, preferences, and practices. Paul is strongly saying such differences between believers should be judged by wise and mature leaders within the church (1 Cor. 6:4).

And even this should be an extreme situation. Resolution and reconciliation should initially be sought privately by following Jesus' commands for settling personal differences (Matt. 18:15–20). Only if that fails should believers "tell it to the church."

Unfortunately, even to this day, property disputes, damage suits, libelous words, unpaid bills or, worse yet, divided churches have dragged believers into court to argue against each other. Always such actions tend to lessen the world's respect for Christians and their churches.

 ### FAITH ALIVE

What bearing do Paul's words to the Corinthian believers have on Christians today?

Are we under the same prohibition regarding litigation against our fellow believers as the Corinthians were? Why?

Have courts of law improved since Paul's day? Does that make any difference?

What if we are not sure the other disputant is truly a believer?

What if a lawsuit is not personal but between your respective insurance companies?

What would you do if you had a serious dispute with another believer which you had tried to reconcile privately, but could not, and now the church leadership will not attempt to arbitrate?

BIBLE EXTRA

Paul entered into direct rebuttal with the prideful believers by reminding them of their union with the Messiah, to whom all judgment is committed (cf. John 5:22; Matt. 19:28; Rev. 20:4). If God would entrust them with that greater responsibility and authority in the coming world, shouldn't they be able to handle rather petty decisions and disputes today?

Who will judge the world? (John 5:22; 1 Cor. 6:2; Rev. 3:21)

Who will judge angels? (1 Cor. 6:3; 2 Pet. 2:4; Jude 6)

Who is qualified to serve as a judge between believers? (1 Cor. 6:4)

Among Christians, Paul said we should be willing to be wronged and cheated rather than to wrong or take advantage of another brother (1 Cor. 6:7, 8). Whether an offense was intentional or unintentional, the spirit of love—which binds true believers together—will insist that we live at peace with our brothers and sisters. It will forbid us to demean ourselves or our faith by going to civil courts of law, which are unlikely to be sensitive to Christian values, motives, or purposes.

FAITH ALIVE

The Association of Christian Conciliation Services[1] has taken seriously Paul's question, "How dare you sue one another?" As a service to the Body of Christ, their Association seeks to train Christians in the art of biblical mediation and/or arbitration. Members' secular training in law or other fields is refined by thorough training in biblical conflict resolution, which enables them to practice the biblical way to resolve legal disputes between believers by serving as mediators rather than prosecutors.

Sam Ericson, a Harvard Law School graduate and the executive director of the Washington, D.C. based Christian Legal Society, offers the following "16 Questions a Christian Should Ask Before Going to Court."[2]

1. What action by me is likely to bring the most glory to God? (1 Cor. 10:23–33)

2. If I had six months left to live, how much of my time would I spend in litigation? (Ps. 90:12)

3. What are my true motives for getting involved in litigation? Is it a desire for revenge or security? (1 Cor. 13; Matt. 5:38–48; 7:1–5)

4. Is there a principle or issue at stake which is broader than my personal interests? (Acts 5:17–32)

5. Will the action I take compromise my witness before other Christians? Will I be a stumbling block? (Rom. 14:13; 1 Tim. 4:12)

6. Will the action I take compromise my witness before non-Christians? Will I be a hindrance to their receiving the gospel? (1 Cor. 6:1–8; 10:32, 33)

7. Will the action I take compromise my witness before the other party, their counsel, or my counsel? (Rom. 15:1-3)

8. Will the action I take compromise the testimony of the church or other Christians? (1 Cor. 6:1–8; 10:32, 33)

9. Will my action have potentially damaging consequences on "innocent" third parties? (Matt. 18:1–6; Mark 9:42; Luke 17:1–5)

10. Does Scripture expressly forbid the action I plan to take? (e.g., Matt. 5:31, 32)

11. Does Scripture expressly endorse the action I plan to take? (Acts 25:1–12)

12. Does the dispute affect my obligations to my family and household? (1 Tim. 5:8)

13. Am I most concerned about my name, reputation, and feelings? (Matt. 5:38–42)

14. What are my other alternatives? (Matt. 5:23–26; 6:8–15; 18:15–18)

  a. Is forgiveness appropriate? [Always!]
  b. Is settlement and compromise appropriate?
  c. Have I met with the person one-on-one to discuss my views and listen to his?
  d. Have I sought out counselors or mediators to assist in reconciliation?

15. Am I as eager to forgive and be reconciled as I am to assert my rights? (Matt. 6:12–15)

16. In whom have I placed my real trust? (Matt. 6:19–34)

PROBING THE DEPTHS

You can study the issues of church discipline further by reading Roy Knuteson's *Calling the Church to Discipline*.[3] He traces discipline through the Old and New Testaments, then explains the principles and steps of discipline in the modern church. Knuteson also emphasizes that there is a right way to discipline within the perimeters of God-given authority.

Insights into the potential for Christians reconciling legitimate differences out of court can be found in Lynn Buzzard and Laurence Eck's *Tell It to the Church*.[4]

And Attorney Carl F. Lansing's *Legal Defense Handbook for Christians in Ministry*[5] will provide guidelines for churches and church organizations in an age of increasing litigation.

Like many believers today, some of the Corinthian Christians were deceived into thinking that personal life-style had little to do with their eternal life. They compartmentalized their beliefs and their behavior. Paul warned them that God would permit no moral compromisers into His kingdom: "Do you not know that the unrighteous will not inherit the kingdom of God? Do not be deceived. Neither fornicators, nor idolaters, nor adulterers, nor homosexuals, nor sodomites, nor thieves, nor covetous, nor drunkards, nor revilers, nor extortioners will inherit the kingdom of God" (1 Cor. 6:9, 10).

After this catalog of coarse sins in verses 9 and 10, Paul presents to the Corinthians—as well as to contemporary Christians—a revolting reminder that "such were some of you" (v. 11). But their transforming conversion "in the name of the Lord Jesus and by the Spirit of our God" made them walking proof of the power of Jesus Christ. They were not the same as they once were. They were now fully cleansed from sin ("washed"), set apart for God ("sanctified"), and totally accepted in His holy sight ("justified").

It is "not by works of righteousness which we have done, but according to His mercy He saved us, through the washing of regeneration" (Titus 3:5). Because we have been treated mercifully we can treat others mercifully (see Gal. 6:1, 2). God is able to forgive and cleanses us from every kind of sin, no matter how great and deep the power of evil is within us.

He then positionally sets us apart "in Christ" for special service as a "temple" (v. 19) or dwelling place for His own nature and Spirit. Like trophies of God's grace, we are to be used only for special, "sanctified" service and distinct display. With such a holy life-style we will bring glory to God with our bodies as well as our spirits (v. 20).

The Judge of heaven and earth has declared us to be just or "not guilty" in His sight. This divine "pardon" is the universal remedy for sin (Rom. 3:24–31). Now we have a fresh start toward becoming what God has already declared us to be! We can begin to live as who we are, rather than as who we once were!

1. Association of Christian Conciliation Services (ACCS), 1537 Avenue D, Suite 352, Billings, MT 59102, (406) 256-1583.

2. Samuel E. Ericson, "16 Questions a Christian Should Ask Before Going to Court" (Washington, D.C., Christian Legal Society, 1987).

3. Roy E. Knuteson, *Calling the Church to Discipline* (Nashville, TN: Action Press, 1977).

4. Lynn R. Buzzard and Laurence Eck, *Tell It to the Church* (Elgin, IL: David C. Cook Publishing Co., 1982).

5. Carl F. Lansing, *Legal Defense Handbook for Christians in Ministry* (Colorado Springs, CO: NavPress, 1992).

Lesson 4/*God Wants Your Body*
(6:12–20)

There is danger in knowledge and truth.

Discovering that we are accepted by God by reason of our faith in the finished work of Christ on the Cross, and not by any religious works of righteousness, is potentially dangerous. We might be tempted to live by the minimum standards, asking what we can get by with, rather than experience the maximum blessings, living in the fullness of God's pathway to purity and power.

The issues of life—in the early church and now—revolve around moral values and ethics. The critical questions concern right and wrong, freedom and responsibility. They reveal spiritual standards and motives.

Ethical decision-making calls for spiritual maturity. Every area of life is now to be sacred and "set apart" for God's glory. Certain activities and issues of life are rather morally indifferent. God may not have said "yes" or "no" about them. Instead, we are left to make decisions based on ethical principles and positions derived from biblical commands, community standards, and personal convictions.

 FAITH ALIVE

How can we avoid being absorbed by secular thinking on "gray areas" of ethical or moral issues? (See Col. 3:3–7; 1 Thess. 4:1–8)

Read Acts 15 and consider the way the early church developed "community standards" on a controversial issue that had no biblical absolutes to apply. What facts can you uncover? What factors were discussed? Who made the final decisions, and what was the effect?

How can personal convictions help us live better lives? (Eph. 4:14) How can personally developed convictions help us preset moral boundaries? (Col. 2:6—3:2)

What should you do if someone else's convictions differ from yours on issues not covered by a clear commandment in Scripture? (Rom. 14:14–23)

PATHWAYS OF PURITY

In the face of this moral dilemma Paul presented believers a basic principle of liberty, with two limitations: "All things are lawful for me, but all things are not helpful. All things are lawful for me, but I will not be brought under the power of any" (v. 12).

The limitations color the principle of liberty. The first shading comes with the question of expediency or profit: "all things are not helpful" (1 Cor. 6:12). To put questionable issues in focus, we might ask the questions, "Is it good for me?" "Will it add a plus quality to my life?"

It is often the "little foxes" that spoil the vine. Spiritual liberty begins with personal discipline over things that are not profitable to us. Life is too short to be consumed with things that do not add positively to our life and service.

The second shading to the principle of liberty is the issue of control. Paul says, in essence, to ask the question, "Will it get control of me, or will it lessen Christ's control of me?" Indulgence in any activity or habit that ultimately has one in its grip is not liberty but slavery. Like the apostle Paul, we should be determined to be mastered only by Christ. The great fact of the Christian faith is that it makes man free *not* to sin. (See 2 Cor. 9:8; Phil. 4:13; 2 Tim. 1:12; Heb. 7:25; Jude 24.)

THE BODY IS FOR GOD

Paul goes on to teach against sexual promiscuity (6:13). Humankind, he said, is more than bodies with physical desires. Every person is basically made for God, and that includes a person's sex drive. He/she will only find total fulfillment for needs and desires (including the sex drive) through knowing, loving, and obeying God.

Another ethical view of the human body is given in verses 14 and 15 when Paul reminds believers that they each make up the "body of Christ." He then asks if any Christian would consciously take a part of Christ and join that part to a prostitute?

Paul answered his own question by saying, "Certainly not!" Sexual intercourse is more than a biological experience or experiment. It is more than just another physical act, like drinking water or sneezing. It involves the communion of life itself and is to be shared only under the covering of a covenant of commitment (Eph. 5:30, 31). If the believer, who is "washed . . . sanctified . . . justified" (6:11) and filled with the Spirit of Christ, would be so crass as to casually commit fornication in what some have termed "recreational sex," he would literally be contaminating the body of Christ by involving Him in immorality. It is an unthinkable proposition, and one of the primary reasons that, for believers, sex sins are worse than others.

BIBLE EXTRA

Sexual sins are worse than others. Pastor Jack Hayford, the senior pastor of The Church On The Way in Van Nuys, California, believes the contention that God sees all sin as the same may sound righteous and reasonable, but "it is absolutely ignorant of the revelation of the Word of God, and it is impractical at every point.

"Keep in mind," he goes on, "I am not saying sexual sins are more difficult for God to forgive. God's forgiveness is unrestricted. But sexual sins are worse in that they are more damaging personally and socially than all other sins.

"Any of these observations, or even a combination of some of them, may be true of other kinds of sin. But I don't believe that any other sin can be said to devastate us so thoroughly as sexual sin.

"1. Sexual sins are worse than others because they stain the deepest part of a person's identity.

2. Sexual sin exploits the deepest aspects of our emotionality.

3. Sexual sin pollutes the fountainhead of our highest creativity.

4. Sexual sin produces guilt that cripples our confidence in God's forgiveness.

5. Sexual sins compromise the foundation of life's deepest human relationship.

6. Sexual sin exposes us to the risk of begetting and conceiving an unsupported human being.

7. Sexual sin increases the probability of multiplying the spread of disease.

8. Sexual sin gives place to appetites that can only beget further unnatural behavior.

9. Sexual sin breaks trust with the whole body of Christ.

10. Sexual sin assaults the pure lordship of Jesus Christ in your life."[1]

The Christian has a responsibility to stay away from sexual sins because Christ bought his body with the highest price ever paid. The Christian's body does not belong to himself; it belongs to God (6:19).

In *The Normal Christian Life*, Watchman Nee illustrated this principle when he told of a fictitious person who had asked a friend to hold his clothes while he went swimming in the river. The clothes-guardian found a wad of money in the pocket of the pants and began handing it out to passersby. The swimmer-owner saw what was happening and began yelling at him to stop. The guardian said he found the money and could do what he wanted with it. The true owner protested that he only intended to let the guardian hold the valuables and had never intended to relinquish ownership. The money still belonged to him!

Similarly, God intends to retain ownership of our lives, which He bought with the blood of His Son on the Cross. We belong to Him and have no right to do as we wish with our lives or our bodies (vv. 19, 20).

FAITH ALIVE

What makes our bodies special? (6:15)

How should this affect how we use them and what we put in them?

When evaluating ethical decisions, how would thinking of yourself as "God's property" affect your considerations? Explain.

AVOIDING PHYSICAL ABUSE

God doesn't forbid fornication because He is against our enjoying the pleasures of life. Rather, God wants to help us avoid a deceptive and destructive form of physical abuse. He does not want people to be used as things instead of persons; He does not want people to be cheated and taken advantage of; He does not want the most intimate of human relationships to be entered into dishonestly and without full and responsible commitment.

Kenneth Chafin appeals for a proper understanding of the value and place of sex: "Sex is being treated as a toy or a plaything. It is being looked upon as a recreational activity, like bowling. The very casual manner in which people who are almost strangers engage in sex has a way of saying, 'It's no big deal.'

"Sex is too important a part of life to be reduced to destructive fun and games. It has tremendous potential for good but used carelessly it can be unbelievably disastrous. I would like for my children to have the feeling that while sex is good it is also extremely important and should be treated accordingly."[2]

PROBING THE DEPTHS

　　What does the Bible say about premarital or extramarital sex?

1 Cor. 6:13–20

1 Cor. 7:2

2 Cor. 11:2

Eph. 5:3–8

Col. 3:15–18

1 Thess. 4:3–5

Heb. 13:4

1 Peter 4:3, 4

　　What biblical counsel could apply to couples involved in "premarital foreplay" while maintaining "technical virginity"?

Rom. 12:1, 2

Rom. 14:13–23

1 Cor. 3:16, 17

Eph. 5:30–32

James 4:7

What does the Bible say about the option of celibacy?

Matt. 19:12

1 Cor. 7:25–34

1 Cor. 10:13

Paul says sexual immorality is sins against our own bodies (6:18). What do you think he meant by that?

How could promiscuous premarital activity become a "habit" (or an appetite, a "felt need") that marriage doesn't break?

Sexual intercourse between unmarried partners—
• Is *biblically wrong* because it violates the clear commandments of God.

• Is *morally wrong* because it can result in broken and twisted lives, unwanted pregnancies, and dreaded venereal diseases.

And perhaps even worse than these reasons, it—

• Is *spiritually wrong* because it provides a "place to the devil" (Eph. 4:27) and a hook that Satan can use to control our lives, limit our influence, and destroy our testimony before our church, our families, and our future children.

Sex is good, right, and pure when it is used according to God's will and plan. It is bad, wrong, and dirty when it is used in selfish, sinful, and irresponsible ways.

The Christian is committed not only to a sound moral code; he is committed above all to the Person of Christ Himself. Therefore, in the face of moral failures in all of society around, a true believer will want to glorify God in his body and spirit (6:20) by always seeking to follow pathways of purity, avoiding fallacious forms of "physical abuse."

---

1. Jack W. Hayford, "Why Sex Sins Are Worse Than Others" (Van Nuys, CA: Living Way Ministries, 1989), audio cassette teaching.

2. Kenneth Chafin, *Is There a Family in the House?* (Waco, TX: Word, Inc., 1978), 127.

Lesson 5/Domestic Difficulties (7:1–40)

The cartoon showed a woman talking to a marriage counselor. She said, "I was looking for an ideal, I married an ordeal, and now I want a new deal!"[1]

We live in an age of "disposable relationships." Marriages are not as permanent as they once were in our society. Recent U.S. Census Bureau statistics suggest that 36% of all first marriages end in divorce. Approximately 80% of those eventually remarry—75% within five years after their divorce. Thirty percent of the second marriages eventually dissolve as well.

Christians are not immune from the heartache of domestic difficulties either. Current studies indicate there to be as high a rate of divorce among proclaiming Christians as among the rest of society.

And the effects of these difficulties and divorces ripple for decades through the lives of children and grandchildren. Family wealth and inheritances have been disrupted and distributed in a different manner than had been planned and developed for decades. School districts and state welfare programs struggle to adjust to the practical dilemmas domestic difficulties dump on society.

GUIDELINES FOR MARITAL INTIMACY
(7:1–9)

In the first six chapters of 1 Corinthians Paul responded to certain reports of confusion and misconduct among the Christians at Corinth. Beginning in chapter 7, he turns his attention to the questions he has received in a letter from someone in the Corinthian church (v. 1). The Corinthians probably did not expect such a long response to their correspondence, but Paul felt these were major issues, especially in light of the morally corrupt city from which the communication came.

He began by responding to various questions pertaining to marriage, human sexuality, and personal relationships. He did not attempt to develop his entire doctrine of marriage in this relatively brief response. That is really only found by studying all of his epistles together. Only when this chapter is taken by itself does misunderstanding and misstatement of his personal and apostolic positions occur.

These were new Christians in a new church saved out of a pagan society. Their entire thinking to this time had been centered in the sinful practices of their ancient religion which was based on immorality. It is not surprising that some other believers were affected by the prevailing practices of their licentious society and desired freedom to express themselves sexually in any way they pleased. They reasoned the spiritual and physical were two mutually exclusive realms or compartments of life. Such a playboy philosophy regarded women as men's playthings and excused the incestuous relationship Paul condemned earlier.

Paul quickly corrected the misapplication of his statement of personal preference by making it clear that marriage was the human norm. He said sexual expression exclusively among married partners was meant by the Creator to counter the temptations and problems of sexual immorality. He completely ruled out any form of extramarital relationships, such as polygamy, homosexuality, adultery, and lesbianism when he specifically said a man was to have his own wife, and a woman was to have her own husband (7:2).

    BIBLE EXTRA

Sex within the bounds of marriage is to be considered beautiful, healthy, and right. One of the reasons people are to marry is to express their sexual nature. But beyond the marriage commitment and without proper self-control, sex is destructive and harmful. The Old Testament laws were very clear about proper sexual relations. Sexuality is to be directly connected to marriage and not to be expressed outside of it (Lev. 18:1–24).

Why should "each man have his own wife"? (1 Cor. 7:2)

What obligations does a Christian wife have toward her husband? (7:4)

To whom does a Christian's body belong if he or she is married? (7:4)

Within marriage there is to be a mutuality of sexual submission (7:3–5). Intimate expression between a husband and wife is, in fact, a Christian *duty* or mutual obligation; a husband is to be available sexually to his wife, and she to him. There should be no sexual selfishness in Christian marriages. Nor is sex to be "used" as a reward or in a manipulative manner.

The physical body is not sinful of itself. The Bible has nothing negative to say about sexual expression between married partners (Song 5:4, 5). Sexual intimacy for Christian couples should be a "holy habit" except for brief periods of time, on condition of common consent and for the sake of special times of fasting or devotion to the Lord. Paul insisted that prolonged abstinence led only to Satanic temptation for one or both partners in sexual fantasy or fact with someone else (1 Cor. 7:5).

 BIBLE EXTRA

Sexual intercourse is an intimate expression of affection between a husband and wife. The apostle underscores its importance in marriage by declaring that it is in fact a *duty:* a

husband is to be available for his wife at her request, and a
wife for her husband at his request.

It is more than an act of biological mating. The Bible
calls it a privileged "mystery" by which two people, a man and
a woman, become one (Eph. 5:32; see Gen. 2:24). The privilege is abused when people not married to each other have
intercourse (1 Cor. 5:1; 6:16): then that which God meant for
blessing becomes a cause of judgment (see Eph. 5:5).

Marriage is the one and the only place that God has
provided for sexual union to take place. In that setting it
becomes a powerful symbol of the love between Christ and
the church, a pure sharing of joy and delight in one another
that is a gift from the hand of God. Outside those boundaries,
it eventually becomes destructive.[2]

The human sex drive is not sinful but natural. Paul wished
all singles and widows could be celibate as he was (v. 8), but he
knew that was unrealistic. Being married or being single is an
individual and relative matter depending in part on one's "gift
from God" (v. 7) and his or her ability to control sexual passion (v. 9). He told the Thessalonians that it was "the will of
God, your sanctification: that you should abstain from sexual
immorality; that each of you should know how to possess his
own vessel in sanctification and honor, not in passion of lust,
like the Gentiles who do not know God" (1 Thess. 4:3–5).

People remain unmarried for different reasons (Matt.
19:11, 12), and each one must know the will of God for them
in that season of their life. Remaining unmarried holds no
superior moral virtue or value. Everyone did not have that
"gift" (v. 7). So, rather than men and women frustrating their
normal sexual drives, it was better to be married.

Marriage is God-ordained (Gen. 2:18–25) and designed
to meet the physical and psychological needs as constituted by
the Creator. That, in part, is why Paul told Timothy that he
desired "the younger *widows* marry, bear children, manage the
house, and give no opportunity to the adversary to speak
reproachfully" (1 Tim. 5:14). Yet, under certain circumstances, Paul told the Corinthians the unmarried person would
be freer to serve the Lord by not having the responsibilities
which go along with married life (7:29–35).

BEHIND THE SCENES

Paul's own marital state has been a matter of considerable speculation. It is clear from verse 8 that Paul was not married. However, some have suggested that he may have been a widower, who lost his wife while yet young. There are perhaps three reasons for this speculation.

First, in Paul's defense before Agrippa (Acts 26) he told of his role in persecuting the believers in Jerusalem. He readily admitted a zeal and madness which resulted in many being imprisoned, persecuted, and even killed. He did this under the authority of the chief priests, "and when they were put to death, I cast my vote against *them*" (v. 10). The fact that he voted in the Sanhedrin indicates to some that he was married, since that was a prerequisite for that position.

Second, chapter 7 seems to be subjective, that is, it seems to have been written by one who knew something of the intimacies and demands of married life. See verses 3–5, 9, 32, 33.

Third, the context of verse 8 is Paul's counsel on the purity of marriage. The "unmarried" who are here paired with the widows, may, in fact, be "widowers" in modern language. It has been observed that there is no word for "widower" in the Greek language. A "widow" *(chera)* was a person "without" or "left without." While a woman might be "left without" a husband and have to await the social functioning of her kinsmen or the affection of a new man, a man could quite easily take steps to obtain a new spouse. A Greek woman left without a spouse was left a "widow," a "person without a source of support." A man in a comparable state was simply a man who chose not to remain "unmarried." Paul's "as I am" in verse 8 may then indicate that he, too, had lost his spouse to death.[3]

Having responded to their questions on the relative morality of marriage and singleness, Paul then turned to the questions of religiously mixed marriages and the possibility of divorce (7:10–16). Because of their desire to serve Christ, some Corinthian Christians thought they ought to divorce their pagan spouses and marry other Christian believers.

Paul affirmed the priority and permanence of the marriage commitment when he said, "A wife is not to depart [separate] from *her* husband. But even if she does depart, let her remain unmarried or be reconciled to *her* husband. And a husband is not to divorce *his* wife" (vv. 10, 11).

PROBING THE DEPTHS

God's original plan was for one man and one woman to separate from their parents and be joined together in a permanent and exclusive union throughout their earthly lives. Divorce was never designed nor desired in the original blueprint for the home. Jesus told the hypocritical Pharisees that "Moses, because of the hardness of your hearts, permitted you to divorce your wives, but from the beginning it was not so" (Matt. 19:8).

If the divine ideal is to create "one flesh" between a husband and wife, is this to be temporary or permanent? (Gen. 2:18–25; Matt. 19:5, 6)

How long are the marriage partners bound to each other? (Rom. 7:2, 3; 1 Cor. 7:39)

If Moses allowed divorce "because of the hardness of your hearts" (Matt. 19:8), are there similar "hardnesses" today? Explain.

According to Paul in 1 Corinthians 7:11, what are a husband and wife to do if marital problems develop and separation or divorce occurs?

KEEP YOUR MARRIAGE VOWS
(7:10–16)

In this section, Paul moved from his advice concerning why a man should get married, to some thoughts on Christian marriage in general and the dilemma of divorce among believers. He endorsed sexual relations within marriage. He heatedly warned against sexual involvement outside of marriage.

First, Paul carefully applied Jesus' prohibition of divorce (Matt. 19:9), stating that a husband and wife should not separate. God's ideal for marriage is that no marriage should be broken. But realizing the reality of human selfishness and societal stresses, he goes on to say that if they do, they should not marry someone else, but rather seek to be reconciled (7:10, 11). Marriage is a sacred bond, and God wants husbands and wives to do nothing to destroy the possibility of reconciliation and restoration of that union.

BIBLE EXTRA

Both Jesus and Paul cited specific circumstances for which divorce is restricted among believers. The primary reason divorce would be allowed is if a believer's mate is guilty of sexual immorality and is unwilling to repent and live faithfully with the marriage partner (Matt. 19:1–9).

The offense of fornication (Gr. *porneia*, from which we get the word "pornography") is used repeatedly in Scripture as a term to describe unlawful, shameful sexual activity. It is an umbrella word denoting intimate sexual involvement, whether that be heterosexual or homosexual, with someone other than one's lawful spouse. If one is married, the sex sin is termed adultery (Ex. 20:14). Sexual sin between singles is included in the larger term of fornication.

Paul made it clear that neither fornicators nor adulterers will enter the kingdom of heaven (1 Cor. 6:9, 10). He saved the good news for the next verse when he reminded the Corinthian saints, "Such were some of you. But you were washed, but you were sanctified, but you were justified in the name of the Lord Jesus and by the Spirit of our God."

It is important to note that even regarding the offense of adultery, divorce is not commanded. It is an option where an unfaithful spouse is not willing to repent and remain faithful to the innocent partner. Yet, in hurt or broken Christian marriages, attempts at reconciliations are always in order. Christians, who do not deserve God's forgiveness in the first place, should be the first to offer human forgiveness to an offending partner who is sincerely repentant.

Paul then went on to give his apostolic advice "to the rest" (of the believers) by applying the Lord's principle to a new area. He, by inspiration of the Holy Spirit, instructs believers on this side of Calvary how to live out what Jesus taught before Calvary (vv. 12–16). God's standards are essentially for believers. The Christian ethic concerning marriage and divorce is only fully possible for those who have the Spirit of Christ helping them in making their marriages succeed.

What is the one essential requirement Paul gives for a Christian in marriage? (7:39)

What is his admonition in 2 Corinthians 6:14? Does it apply to marriage?

What does Ephesians 5:21–33 teach as the best defense against divorce?

Paul's personal applications extend to the failures of religiously mixed marriages. The Christian husband should not leave—literally "separate from" or "divorce"—his non-Christian wife, and the Christian wife should not leave her non-Christian husband (7:12, 13). To Paul, the reason is simple: the holy influence of the believer's life on the unbelieving partner. It might be that the Christian can lead the unsaved mate—and the entire household—to the Lord. (See Gen. 30:27; 39:5; 1 Pet. 3:1, 2.)

DIVORCE FOR DESERTION

But what if the unsaved partner does not want to stay with the one who becomes the Christian? What if he or she prefers pagan ways and wants to leave? Paul says a believer may acquiesce to (not initiate, encourage, or cause) the desertion of an unbelieving partner resulting in irreconcilable separation or divorce (v. 15). The believing partner is a victim of willful desertion or abandonment and not "bound" to the marriage vows in such a case.

The point is that the Christian wife or husband should not attempt to keep a marriage to an unbeliever going if it is continually torn by strife, tension, arguing, and even physical abuse. In such conditions, the non-Christian mate is "departing" or "deserting" the marriage vows ("to love, honor, and cherish"). If the unbeliever wants out of the marriage, the believer is to release him/her, for God has called us to live in peace. "When an unbeliever initiates divorce beyond a believer's control, the believer is free from the relationship, and is not under bondage to keep it intact. Paul is silent concerning remarriage in such a situation."[4]

LIVE AS GOD CALLED YOU
(7:17–24)

The key point in all decisions is in verse 17. The Christian should seek to put his past "in the past" and continue in the same condition of life as when he was called to God's service (vv. 17–24). "Be sure, in deciding these matters," Paul seems to be saying, "that you are living as God intended: marrying or not marrying in accordance with God's direction and help and accepting whatever situation in which God has placed you." No circumstance of life is beyond God's transforming power. A believer's presence may be the purifying element needed to effect kingdom purposes in lives, marriages, and even work environments.

This is Paul's rule for all the churches (v. 17b). He echoes the clear teaching of Christ as he makes it plain that God's ideal for marriage is that no marriage should be broken.

 PROBING THE DEPTHS

Have you developed personal convictions about these delicate matters? Do you believe the Bible allows for divorce? If so, under what circumstances? What about remarriage? What about after we are Christians? What does the Scripture say about issues such as marriage, separation, divorce, and remarriage? Use the following references as a separate study to probe the depths of these crucial scriptures. Come to your own conclusion as a result of this study: Genesis 2:18–25; Deuteronomy 24:1–4; Malachi 2:10–16; Matthew 5:31, 32; 19:3–12; Mark 10:2–12; Romans 7:1–6; 1 Corinthians 7:10–24, 39; Ephesians 5:22–33; 1 Peter 3:1–7.

Never underestimate the power of prayer to change troubled marriages. Prayer is often the only way to discover God's answer to an unhappy marriage.

Reality forces one to acknowledge—especially with today's "no-fault" divorce laws—that even Christian marriages are often legally dissolved for very subjective reasons rather than the biblical bases of adultery (Matt. 19:9) or desertion (1 Cor. 7:15). In such cases, the unwilling partner has few scriptural options. What are they?

Matt. 5:32

1 Cor. 7:10

1 Cor. 7:39, 40

DEALING WITH THE DIVORCED

Some would treat divorce as the "unpardonable sin." Murderers, thieves, and felons can be accepted as forgiven sinners and integrated into the life and service of the church, but—all too often—not the divorced. This is especially true if it is obvious that the divorce was obtained on other than biblical grounds, or if the divorced person has since married someone else. Such persons are sometimes seen to be "living in a state of adultery."

On the other hand, some would treat divorce lightly as a matter of personal choice. Some professing Christians have even deluded themselves to think they could divorce their respective mates and marry each other, because "God understands, and will forgive us." This presumes on the grace and mercy of God. His standards are not to be toyed with! (See Matt. 5:31, 32; 19:4–9.) There should be neither divorce nor cause for divorce in a Christian home—or church.

In some instances the local church may be to blame for divorces. Paul has earlier taken the Corinthian church to task for winking at sexual sin within their ranks and failing to discipline the failing party. When divorce occurs between professing believers, someone is in clear disobedience to God's Word and will. The Christian marriage was meant for life (1 Cor. 7:39). It is to illustrate to the world the commitment and love of Jesus for His bride, the church (Eph. 5:24, 25, 32). Society's rejection of God's standards for marriage, and willing accommodation of divorce by the church, have allowed the enemy a foothold in many Christian fellowships. Church discipline (as in 1 Cor. 5:9—6:10) is clearly called for to restore confidence and credibility in many local churches and their leadership.

Divorce, even when on biblical grounds, is always occasioned by someone's sin. At best then, divorce always brings misery and hurt. That is one of the reasons God hates it (Mal. 2:14–16). However, this strong statement of hatred is directed neither at the divorced one nor at the divorcing one. It is directed solely at divorce itself.

REMARRIAGE AFTER DIVORCE

Moses permitted divorce (and remarriage) because of

hardness of heart (Deut. 24:1–4; Matt. 19:8). The practice of divorce and remarriage among God's people is a tragic reality that carries through to our present day.

As has been observed earlier, the biblical dissolution of marriage may come about in any of three ways according to the Word of God: (1) death of a spouse (1 Cor. 7:39, 40); (2) sexual immorality, *porneia* (Matt. 5:32; 19:9); (3) desertion or abandonment (1 Cor. 7:15). God only acknowledges the dissolution of the marriage vows on His terms.

 BIBLE EXTRA

- "But what about divorce prior to salvation?"
- "Or marital infidelity after salvation?"
- "Or what if professing believers get divorced for non-biblical reasons?"
- "What role or ministry can a divorced person have within a local church?"

These are the kinds of questions which have separated believers and divided churches for centuries. Often, there are no easy answers. Truth must frequently be sought and expressed with great compassion on a case by case basis.

Consider the following verses along with the scriptures in the "Probing the Depths" section earlier, and try to come to your own biblical convictions on these matters. See 1 Corinthians 6:9–11; 7:20; 2 Corinthians 5:17; and 1 John 1:9, 10.

Above all, seek the counsel of your pastor and church leaders on these and other life-issues of this consequence.

A church, as a fellowship of forgiven sinners, should provide a model of redemption for those who are hurt and torn by the tragedy of divorce, whether they are innocent victims, guilty parties, or the families of either. Showing genuine love (which sometimes must be evidenced as "tough love"), acceptance, and forgiveness, congregations should do all they can to seek to help build strong marriages. Biblical principles for marriage and sexual ethics should be taught in sermons and lessons, at seminars and retreats, as well as modeled by the church staff and leadership.

Relationships will get whole when people get whole. Many believe that through the healing work of the Holy Spirit, the forgiveness and grace of God can, in time, open the doors to potential remarriage.

PROBING THE DEPTHS

The Mosaic writing of divorcement completely severed the marriage "bond" (Gen. 2:24) and so dissolved the marriage relationship that the woman was allowed to go and become another man's wife (Deut. 24:4). Jesus approved the Jewish divorce only for the cause of fornication (Matt. 19:9). He did not abolish divorce nor introduce a new kind of divorce. He did correct the abuse of the divorce privilege by the clear restriction "for fornication."

A subsequent remarriage after a Jewish divorce was assumed, and indirectly approved, by both Moses and Jesus (Deut. 24:1–4; Matt.19:9). There are those who likewise see the scriptural possibility of remarriage for a believer who has faced the devastating realities of divorce today.[5] Some have even called the possibility of remarriage after divorce a "healing gift from God."[6]

No remarriage should be rushed. Emotional and psychological healing may be needed over a period of time after a divorce. Even the "innocent" partner in a divorce needs to review the roots of the broken relationship and take responsibility for any failure on their part in fulfilling God's ideal. Lack of an intimate relationship with God and certain selfish tendencies may have contributed in some degree to the marriage failure.

Prayerful counsel from elders in the local church and a reasonable period of time for emotional healing are wise prerequisites before any thoughts of remarriage. All the while, the "suddenly single" will be faced with resisting the temptations of the flesh while focusing new time and energy on serving Christ and His church. (See 1 Cor. 7:26–35.)

ADVICE AND ADVANTAGES FOR STAYING SINGLE
(7:25–40)

In this final section of instruction on marriage and sexual ethics Paul spoke of a soon-coming time of persecution and distress; then he dealt with service to the Lord in light of Christ's imminent return. Also, Paul developed the concept that singles have fewer distractions from time spent on spiritual matters than those who are married and have family responsibilities.

There is no escaping it; marriage is a challenge. Paul wanted to debunk the theory that one can be happy and fulfilled only when married. There are definite and distinct advantages of being single, not the least of which is the opportunity to place a greater focus on Christ and His work (vv. 32–35).

Though he suggested that marriages might be better put off "because of the present distress" (v. 26), they were not prohibited. Paul let the believers know that God will guide differently in some individual cases. Believers will not sin if they marry or if they remain single.

 FAITH ALIVE

What are some advantages of being single?

What are some advantages of being married?

What opportunities do married people have that single people do not have?

How can you use your unique experiences as a married
or single person in service to God?

Finally, many mature Christians believe the specific restriction for widows to marry "only in the Lord" (v. 39) is likewise prudent for all believers (2 Cor. 6:14). Only then can a couple be mutually "submitted" to each other and to the Lord (Eph. 5:21–33). Peter gives guidance to wives whose husbands are unbelievers, but how much better for them both to be drawing on the power of the Holy Spirit in their lives and benefiting as "heirs together of the grace of life" (1 Pet. 3:1–7).

1. *So You're Getting Married,* by H. Norman Wright. Copyright © 1985. Regal Books, Ventura, CA 93003, 10. Used by permission.

2. *Spirit-Filled Life Bible* (Nashville, TN: Thomas Nelson Publishers, 1991), 1727, "Kingdom Dynamics: Three Sides of Sex."

3. Taken from the book, MAN AND WOMAN IN BIBLICAL PERSPECTIVE by James B. Hurley, 137, 138. Copyright © 1981 by James B. Hurley. Used by permission of Zondervan Publishing House.

4. *Spirit-Filled Life Bible,* 1728, note on 7:15.

5. Ken Stewart, *Divorce and Remarriage* (Tulsa, OK: Harrison House, Inc., 1984).

6. Larry Richards, *Remarriage: A Healing Gift from God* (Waco, TX: Word Books, 1981).

Lesson 6/Christian Ethics (8:1—11:1)

The news report seemed out of place in today's permissive society. An ultraconservative denomination was reported as reaffirming a strict code of behavior for its 500,000-member fellowship. It was on record as requiring its ministers to recommit to a conduct code prohibiting "mixed swimming, television, women with short hair or makeup, dancing, worldly amusements and sports, immodest dress, theater attendance, and unwholesome music." Church officials said the rigid restrictions are based on the Bible, and the denomination's 7,500 ministers had 90 days to decide whether to resign or reaffirm their commitment.[1]

The categories may seem more modern, but the root issues are the same as Paul was essentially asked in 1 Corinthians 8: "What ethics should govern a Christian's life-style?" "How can a Christian remain in this world and not be compromised by its values?"

A MATTER OF CONSCIENCE
(8:1–12)

The questions came to Paul out of a difference of opinion in the church at Corinth about whether or not it was permissible for a Christian to eat food which had been sacrificed in a pagan religious ceremony. This was a rather routine ritual in Paul's day, and much confusion and division in the Gentile church resulted from the practice. For instance, did it really make a difference whether the meat had been part of a pagan sacrifice? Did it matter where they ate the meat (in a public or private setting)? If meat had this questionable connotation, should they eat meat at all, or become vegetarians?

The Corinthians appealed to Paul to settle this social dispute and tell them who was right or wrong concerning this practical matter. His response is insightful for modern believers who face contemporary conduct and consciences and need guidance in resolving disputed issues that threaten to divide believers.

Paul was careful not to give either side satisfaction at first. Instead, he sought to guide them with principles of discernment and discipleship. Each side based its conviction that *it* was right on an appeal to revealed truth and on the belief that it had a better grasp of truth than the other side. Paul began with a warning. "Knowledge puffs up [makes arrogant], but love edifies [builds up]" (8:1). Each side had some understanding or "knowledge" of God's truth (v. 1), but to focus on facts of knowledge alone will only develop spiritual pride. Thus, an arrogant attitude is a false foundation for solving doctrinal debates.

> Eating food is essentially an ethically neutral act (v. 8), but not all people have the same level of knowledge. Some new converts were uncertain about the power of their former pagan gods; others knew idols held no power over them. Knowledge has two defects: it tends to center on self, and it is inadequate as the bond in personal relationships. The obligations of love are the determining factor in questions of moral insignificance. The principle of love places limitations on one's liberty of conscience.[2]

Paul then added to his analysis of the debate. Not only must knowledge be tempered by love, but love must make one sensitive to the relational results of applying that knowledge. Orthodoxy in one truth does not excuse ignoring application of another. "But food does not commend us to God; for neither if we eat are we the better, nor if we do not eat are we the worse. But beware lest somehow this liberty of yours become a stumbling block to those who are weak" (vv. 8, 9).

Verse 8 implies that a weak brother lacks personal biblical knowledge. He has been spoon-fed his biblical knowledge and opinions by others, and he has not studied to present himself "approved to God, a worker who does not need to be ashamed, rightly dividing the word of truth" (2 Tim. 2:15). Because of this lack of biblical knowledge, the Devil has a field day as the great "accuser of the brethren." He works with the weak believer's oversensitive conscience and condemns him for things the Scriptures would suggest are permissible.

The weak believer is often influenced by the actions or opinions of stronger Christians who are fully convinced in their own personal convictions and live their lives in the liberty of their positions. His own underdeveloped convictions make him vulnerable to Satan's condemnation or to a critical spirit toward those believers who are convinced in their convictions. The "weak believer" may not be only newer converts, but believers from another country or culture who have difficulty adjusting to the ethics and practices of other "brothers and sisters."[3]

 FAITH ALIVE

Paul summarizes his teaching on Christian liberties in Romans 14 by stressing the need for each one to be fully convinced in his own mind what the will of God is for him in areas where God's will is not specific in His Word. In nonessentials, "gray areas" of Christian ethics, personal convictions are essential in being free from needless guilt and sin. He makes three points: (1) personal convictions are "personal"; (2) personal convictions are to be practiced; and (3) personal convictions must be developed.

Read Romans 14:13–15. What words describe how our actions might affect another believer?

Is it difficult for you to set aside your liberties in Christ for someone else's spiritual good? Explain when you did this last.

Who was the ultimate example in setting aside his rights for the good of someone else? (14:15) Explain.

How could our exercising Christian liberties discredit the "work of God"? (14:20)

Does this mean we must forever limit our liberties? If so, are they really liberties?

Which are you? A "weak" believer or a "strong" believer? Why?

Who among your friends is "weak"? What factors maintain this position in their lives?

Why are your personal convictions to be kept between you and God? (v. 22)

What will happen if you participate in some amusement, recreation, or social activity that you are not fully convinced is okay for you? (v. 23)

Can you think of a recent time when you did not practice your own personal convictions? What happened?

DEVELOPING PERSONAL CONVICTIONS

Personal convictions must be personally developed. To have lasting value they cannot be borrowed from someone else, nor force-fed by someone else. They must become the daily standards by which life is lived with integrity and honesty before God. Fuzzy consciences become clear by consistently applying biblical principles. Make sure the convictions you develop are based on the Word of God and not just an effort to rationalize your selfish desires.

 FAITH ALIVE

Consider the following principles and questions to help in developing your own personal convictions. Objectively apply *all* the following "guidelines for gray areas" to a given issue before deciding if the matter in question is right or wrong for you.

1. PROFIT (1 Cor. 6:12). Ask the questions: "Is it good for me?" "Will it add a plus quality to my life?"

2. CONTROL (1 Cor. 6:12). Ask the questions: "Will it get control of me, or will it lessen Christ's control of me?"

3. OWNERSHIP (1 Cor. 6:19, 20). Consider the questions: "As God's property, can I justify this activity? Is this activity befitting an ambassador of Jesus Christ?"

4. INFLUENCE (1 Cor. 8:9, 12, 13). "Could this action negatively influence any of my friends or cause them to stumble?"

5. TESTIMONY (Col. 4:5). Now consider: "How will my testimony be affected if I participate in this activity?"

6. THANKSGIVING (Col. 3:17). Reflect on this question: "When I come home from this activity, can I thank God for it with a clear conscience?"

7. LOVE (Rom. 14:13–15). As the final question, ask: "Am I willing to limit my liberties in loving consideration of another?"

A PATTERN OF SELF-DENIAL
(9:1–27)

In deciding doubtful and debatable questions, Paul moved from the "Law of Conscience" to the "Law of Charity." To take advantage of our liberties in Christ (2 Cor. 3:17b; James 2:12) at the expense of deliberately wounding or weakening another's conscience is wrong. Love should overrule liberty (8:9; 1 Pet. 2:16b). Paul taught this principle in chapter 8, illustrated it in chapter 9 and applied it in chapter 10.

The principles of Christian liberty and their limits are illustrated in chapter 9 when Paul uses his life and ministry as an example. He shared how he had voluntarily chosen to surrender many of his own "rights" so as not to harm his relationships with the Corinthians. His apostolic office entitled him to certain privileges, but he renounced them for their sake. Had he insisted on these rights, others might have been offended, his motives could have been questioned, and the work of Christ may have been hindered.

The Corinthians had been saying that because they were "mature" and "strong" believers, they were free to do whatever they wanted. They wouldn't participate in the pagan religious ceremonies, but they were certainly free afterward to eat the meat that had been sacrificed. After all, they were liberated people.

So Paul began with that premise and proclaimed he was likewise a mature believer. He even claimed to be an authenticated apostle! He had seen the resurrected Christ, not only on the Damascus Road on his way to persecute Christians (Acts 9:3–6), but also in a night vision right there in Corinth (Acts 18:9, 10). And if that were not enough, they could look to themselves. They were the attestation of his apostleship. They were the fruit of of his labor, the "seal" witnessing to the effectiveness of his work as an apostle (1 Cor. 9:2).

 FAITH ALIVE

What is attractive to you about Paul's freedom?

Have you ever tried to exert your freedom by rebelling against authority? If so, how did God deal with you about it?

Do others find grace and freedom in your attitudes and actions?

If anyone wanted to investigate Paul they would find he had as many, if not more, rights as the best of them. But he had voluntarily withheld demanding those rights, and even asking for reasonable support from them. He had a right to seek support from them in the way of meals (Luke 10:1–9; 1 Tim. 5:18), as well as support for a wife. Cephas (Peter) had already evidenced the reasonableness and right of an apostle to have a wife and to travel in ministry together and receive support from those to whom they ministered (1 Cor. 9:3–6). As a farmer eats of his crops and flocks, Paul insisted he had a right to financial support from the flock he shepherded (vv. 7, 8). God's people should have cared for God's servant as surely as the law of Moses cared for the oxen that threshed (v. 9).

By these examples Paul is teaching that those who work for the sake of the gospel should expect to benefit from that labor. Paul's spiritual work with the Corinthians should result in material support from them. The Old Testament priests received tithes (v. 13), and in the New Testament "the Lord has commanded that those who preach the gospel should live from the gospel" (v. 14). The church has the responsibility to support its leaders, pastors, teachers, evangelists, and missionaries; and they have the right to ask for that support (1 Tim. 5:17, 18).

Paul had the right to receive the support from the church, but he also had the liberty to refuse it, which he did (1 Cor. 9:15). He became an example of someone who sets aside a "right" so others would have nothing to criticize, thus removing one more obstacle for the gospel. By refusing remuneration from the church, he did not relieve the Corinthians of their responsibility; he merely circumvented it by his "right" to not demand his "rights." He was free to take their money, but he made himself a "servant to all, that I might win the more" (v. 19). His genuine love for others motivated him to limit his liberty for the sake of others.

Some people see things as either black or white. The tyranny of peer pressure keeps them locked in dead traditions of the past rather than finding fresh ways to minister the Bread of Life to others. Paul was secure in who he was in Christ, and that allowed him great freedom to be creative in his witness to others. Being flexible in his approach to ministry, he offended neither Gentile nor Jew (vv. 20, 21).

Paul lived his life like an athlete who runs a race—to win. He had a focused purpose and disciplined his life, giving up what was good, or even better, to gain the best. Having clear goals and priorities, he gave up his rights, even his right to legitimate income, to win an incorruptible crown. Successful Christian living and ministry does not happen by accident. It comes to those disciplined disciples (even apostles!) who are willing to limit their liberties in order to be used by God.

 FAITH ALIVE

Is there anything in your life that might hinder the spread of the gospel? Talk to God about this.

Is there a liberty you are holding onto that is causing this hindrance?

If so, what steps can you take to remove this hindrance?

When and how will you begin to do so?

LESSONS FROM HISTORY
(10:1–11)

Moving from his own life as an example of balanced discipline, Paul now reverts in chapter 10 to Hebrew history to illustrate the dangers, as well as delights, of spiritual freedoms. The nation of Israel was free from Egyptian bondage and had many privileges, but they did not discipline themselves nor limit their liberties. They abused their liberty with self-indulgence, and their actions affected generations to follow. Their failures in the wilderness wanderings serve as examples to modern pilgrims (v. 6).

Paul began by listing five great events of Israel's redemptive history (vv. 1–5). Answering the related questions below will focus our attention on the lessons to be learned.

1. God provided supernatural guidance: "all our fathers were under the cloud" (v. 1). How did the cloud guide them? (Ex. 13:21, 22)

2. God provided a supernatural deliverance: "all passed through the sea" (v. 1). What happened to the enemy armies? (Ex. 14:21, 22)

3. God provided a supernatural unity: "all were baptized into Moses in the cloud and in the sea" (v. 2). How did the people show their commitment to Moses' authority and leadership? (Ex. 14:30, 31)

4. God provided a supernatural food: "all ate the same spiritual [or supernatural] food" (v. 3). How often was the manna supplied? (Ex. 16:4, 15, 35)

5. God provided a supernatural drink: "and all drank the same spiritual drink. For they drank of that spiritual Rock that followed them, and that Rock was Christ" (v. 4). Even in the desert the Hebrews received needed provisions from the pre-incarnate Presence (Ex. 17:1–7). Will He still meet our needs today? (Phil. 4:13; Heb. 13:8)

If there is a lesson to be learned from these examples it is that spiritual privileges do bring increased responsibilities, but they do not guarantee spiritual success. One would think that after all these special blessings of supernatural direction, deliverance, and diet the people would respond with genuine thankfulness and careful obedience. This was not the case with them, nor is it with many modern believers. After listing these blessings from God, Paul says bluntly: "With most of them God was not well pleased" (10:5). They had everything going for them, but they were undisciplined in their freedoms and disqualified themselves.

Many modern Christians face the same dangers with a kind of "spiritual saturation." They have various versions of the Bible, along with study guides and commentaries to fully educate in the Word. Then they have "apostles, prophets, and pastor-teachers" on radio, television, and in their mailboxes. They have summer camps and seminars; satellite dishes and cassettes in cars. *Everything* you need for spiritual growth is available. In such a privileged environment modern saints easily get spoiled and occasionally become sour. We do well to learn these lessons from our spiritual ancestors and thereby avoid repeating their mistakes (vv. 6, 11). As someone has said, those who fail to learn from history are condemned to repeat it.

PROBING THE DEPTHS

What were five directions Paul gave to the haughty Hebrews?

1. 10:6

2. 10:7

3. 10:8

4. 10:9

5. 10:10

 FAITH ALIVE

Is it possible to put something ahead of God and make an idol out of it? Has that happened in your life? Identify it and confess it to God.

Have you ever "tempted Christ" by seeing how far you could go to the edge of Christian ethics? Have you repented of this sin?

Immorality begins with an attitude and progresses to an action. Have you allowed a lax attitude that is inconsistent with purity?

Are there specific things you need to renounce now so you can be clean before God and not give a "place to the devil"? (Eph. 4:27) Explain:

When you don't get what you want from God when you want it, do you find it easy to complain and be "mad at God"?

AVOIDING AND OVERCOMING TEMPTATION
(10:12, 13)

Paul seemed concerned the Corinthians were irresponsible in their Christian "freedoms" and were setting themselves up for a fall. So he gave them some very pointed and practical advice in verses 12 and 13 of chapter 10—a warning and a promise that are still valuable today. He told them they needed to be realistic both about the trials they faced and their own strength to resist. Thinking one is too mature and too spiritual to be tempted or to fall is nothing but spiritual pride. No one is immune to such failure.

Good people are daily being seduced by sensual desires and materialism. Their years of experience and biblical knowledge seem no match against the "wiles of the devil" (Eph. 6:11). Paul's advice is for believers to avoid temptation by distinguishing between assurance and overconfidence (v. 12).

Wrong desires and temptations are faced by everyone. They are not unusual. Throughout human experience believers have learned to recognize the source of these temptations and to resist them. God's Word and God's Spirit are ready resources to assist the sincere Christian in resisting "the world, the flesh, and the devil."

AVOID THE SEDUCTION OF IDOLATRY
(10:14–22)

Like Joseph, deliberate avoidance is often the best defense against temptation. Paul uses a strong command to warn the Corinthians to run away from pagan religious festivities: "Flee from idolatry" (v. 14). The actual idol may be nothing (8:4), but the demonic powers behind it are real, and the act of worship of an idol is not a meaningless act but involves one with demonic forces (10:20). Paul tactfully suggested that he expected the Corinthians, as wise and prudent people, to understand and appreciate why he wanted them to avoid any compromise in this sensitive area.

Just as believers commune with Christ in the Lord's supper (vv. 16, 17) and reaffirm the Covenant's provisions by sharing in the elements of communion, so sharing food as a part of a pagan festival involves fellowship with demons (v. 20; Deut. 32:17, 21). Demonic forces are the resources Satan uses against us (Eph. 6:12). Believers are to fight against them, not have fellowship with them through unwitting compromise.

ANALYZING THE AMORAL AND THE IMMORAL (10:23—11:1)

Another principle of Christian ethics is that an action that is essentially *amoral* can become functionally *immoral* in a certain context. Paul provides that context when he presents practical possibilities for contact with meat that had been offered to idols. He had already made clear that joining with pagans in religious ceremonies that involved eating meat sacrificed to the demon deities in their temples was wrong and would inevitably "provoke the Lord to jealousy" (10:19–22).

The next context is in shopping for meat in butchers' stalls at the local meat market (v. 25). Meat sacrificed to idols was still meat made by the one true God for the good and sustenance of man, for "the earth *is* the LORD's and all its fullness" (v. 26). Therefore, if the price was right, the believer could buy it and enjoy it without making an issue of it. An action that is essentially *amoral* is allowable.

However, if that same meat were offered as food in a friend's house it might be considered differently. Freely practicing matters that are essentially *amoral* might well depend on the circumstances. At a common meal they were advised to willingly eat "whatever is set before you, asking no questions for conscience' sake" (v. 27). But if a weaker Christian made an issue of it, saying, "This was offered to idols," then they should leave it alone so as not to be a problem to the conscience of the one with underdeveloped biblical convictions (vv. 28, 29).

Paul extended that duty to the Jews and Greeks, as well as the fellow church members (v. 32). Biblical knowledge and Christian freedom are not to be selfishly used. Rather, godly love is to compel and motivate all believers and draw many to salvation (v. 33). Paul invited the Corinthians (and all Christians) to follow his example in this unselfish life-style.

1. "National & International Religion Report" (Roanoke, VA: Media Management), Vol. 7, No. 4 (February 8, 1993), 2.

2. *Spirit-Filled Life Bible* (Nashville, TN: Thomas Nelson Publishers, 1991), 1730, note on 8:1.

3. Gary Friesen, *Decision Making and the Will of God* (Questar: Multnomah Books, 1980).

Lesson 7/Another Limit to Liberty (11:2–16)

Over the period of years after Paul began the ministry in Corinth, the church developed many problems. In earlier portions of this epistle the apostle discussed matters of division, lack of discipline, domestic life, and the duty of believers to the Lord and to one another.

Beginning in this chapter, Paul addresses another problem, one that involved the decorum or behavior of believers as they met for worship. The situation had apparently gotten out of hand, and Paul devoted a major portion of this letter (chs. 11—14) to dealing with these matters of disorder in church conduct. There were three areas of concern: (1) the tendency to defy social custom and dishonor God-given authority (11:2–16); (2) the cliquishness marring the Lord's Supper (11:17–34); and (3) the misuse of spiritual gifts (chs. 12—14).

ANOTHER LIMIT TO LIBERTY

Although many ancient cultures and religions considered women to be inferior to men, the Bible, on the other hand, nowhere belittles women or regards them as inferior to men. On the contrary, women are exalted in the Bible and are to be treated with great consideration and honor (1 Pet. 3:7). Clear statements such as Paul sets out in Galatians 3:28 establish the norm for all other passages: "There is neither male nor female; for you are all one in Christ Jesus."

This liberating element to the Christian doctrine has greatly enlarged the role of Christian women in all facets of life, including Christian worship. The general Greek culture reflected the common feeling that women were inferior to men—not quite as low as animals perhaps, but not on a par with man either. The taste of spiritual liberty and equality was sweet to the Corinthian women, and some sought to express it by rejecting established religious customs—including some traditions taught by Paul, the founding pastor.

The first problem Paul approached was the rebellious attitude of some of the women toward head coverings and authority. He taught that "every woman who prays or prophesies with *her* head uncovered dishonors her head, for that is one and the same as if her head were shaved" (1 Cor. 11:5).

FAITH ALIVE

What did Paul mean in this verse?

What does this mean to modern believers?

Does Paul seem to acknowledge women praying and prophesying in the Corinthian congregation? Is this significant?

What are some ways that women today struggle to symbolize their equality with men?

Which, if any, of these issues involve a denial of the identity and value of women?

What differences between men and women should be acknowledged?

Do these differences make one sex of lesser/greater importance? Why/why not?

Do you think that we Christians and our churches as a rule give true recognition to the worth and value of women? Why/why not?

PROPER CONDUCT IN PUBLIC WORSHIP
(11:2–16)

Before correcting their errors, Paul began by praising the Corinthian church for keeping many of the "traditions" he had taught (1 Cor. 11:2; 2 Thess. 2:15). Then he proceeded to correct their public behavior with seven distinct areas of argument.

1. *He appealed to God's created order (v. 3).* It is clear from apostolic teaching that God has established a hierarchy of headship to maintain order and authority in personal, family, church, and civil matters (Rom. 13:1–7; Heb. 4:14–16; 13:7; 1 Pet. 2:13, 14). So Paul began by reminding the Corinthians about God's "chain of command" for the home: "I want you to know that the head of every man is Christ, the head of woman *is* man, and the head of Christ *is* God" (v. 3).

Why did God establish man as the family head?

What does this say about the relative intelligence/wisdom of women?

BEHIND THE SCENES

In the Old Testament the word "head" (Heb., *ro'sh*) had many meanings. Among them: (1) the source or beginning, as of a river; (2) the top, as of a mountain; (3) a chief or ancestral head of a family or clan; or (4) highest rank in the military, judicial, or other hierarchy.[1]

In the New Testament, the word (Gr., *kephaie*) is used in either an organic or organizational context. By Paul's day the primary metaphorical meanings of the word could be a person with authority over something/someone, or the source of something/someone.

PROBING THE DEPTHS

Examine each of the passages and questions below and describe from the context the theologically significant uses of "head" as either "authority over" or "source of."

Who is the head of all creation and the church? (Eph. 1:20–23)

Who is the head of the church? (Eph. 1:22; 4:15; 5:23; Col. 1:18; 2:10, 19)

Who is the head of Jesus? (1 Cor. 11:3b)

Who is the source/head of spiritual growth? (Eph. 4:15)

Who is the head of the wife? (Eph. 5:22–33)

Who is the head of man, and who is the head of woman? (1 Cor. 11:3)

Is one superior? Is one inferior? (1 Cor. 11:11, 12) Explain.

Head coverings were at issue in 1 Corinthians 11. These were not understood as having anything to do with woman's origin from man. Rather they were cultural symbols of her relation to her husband's authority. The type of head covering is not specified, merely the importance of the wife's head being covered as a then-cultural-signal of respect for her husband and reverence for Christ. For in spite of the fact that the man prayed without a head covering, he still has a Head and that is Christ (v. 3).

BEHIND THE SCENES

Jack Hayford has made a significant observation in defining "man" as used in verse 3: "*Anthropos* occurs over 500 times in the New Testament. It's the most common word for 'man,' referring to man as (1) the male of the species, or (2) to a mankind as a race. It is used both ways.

"But far more specific in designating 'man' is the word *aner,* which occurs here. *Aner* appears about 250 times in the Greek New Testament; and about 50 of those times it is translated 'husband.' Thus, when it's put together, this passage is clearly describing a husband-wife relationship. . . ."[2]

The Bible does not assign rigid social or church roles to men and women on a gender basis alone. Women are not required to show special respect to all men everywhere, but rather to their own husbands. When a woman chooses to become married, she brings herself under her husband's biblical responsibility and authority and is commanded to live her life in reverential submission to him (1 Pet. 3:1–7). The passage (11:3) should be understood as a reference to husbands and wives rather than a gender reference in general. The husband was to be respected as the "head" for his domestic and economic roles and responsibilities under God's creative order as the protector, provider, and priest of the home.

FAITH ALIVE

How does understanding his wife's vulnerabilities help a husband protect her? (1 Pet. 3:7)

What does the Bible say about someone who does not provide for his family? (1 Tim. 5:8)

How would the husband's role as the family "head" be lived out as part of the holy priesthood? (1 Pet. 2:4, 5)

How does Christ's example prepare the husband for his role as the spiritual leader of the home? (Eph. 5:23–30)

BIBLE EXTRA

Jesus and the Father Model Relationship for Marriage (11:3). The relationship between God as "Head" and Christ as Son is given as a model for the relationship between husband and wife. When the Bible reveals how the Father and the Son relate to each other, it also tells us something about the way husbands and wives should relate to each other.

The following principles for governing husband-wife relationships are illustrated in the relationship of Jesus and the Father: 1) Husband and wife are to share a mutual love (John 5:20; 14:31). 2) Husband and wife have different roles and accomplish different functions in the marriage (John 10:17; 14:28; 17:4). 3) Though having different roles, husband and wife are equal; they live in unity (John 10:30; 14:9,11). 4) Husband and wife esteem one another (John 8:49, 54). 5) Husbands express love for their wives through care, shared life and ministry, and attentiveness (John 5:20,

22; 8:29; 11:42; 16:15; 17:2). 6) Wives express love for their husbands by being of one will and purpose with them; by exercising authority entrusted to them with humility and meekness, not striving or competing; in a word, by showing <u>respect</u> both in attitude and action (John 4:34; 5:19, 30; 8:28; 14:31; 15:10; Phil. 2:5, 6, 8; see also Gen. 3:16; 1 Tim. 2:8–15).[3]

2. *Paul appealed to the appropriateness of following certain social customs (1 Cor. 11:4–6).* The church at Corinth was primarily a Gentile congregation. The social custom of that society was for men to have their heads uncovered and the women to cover theirs in public. This was the opposite of the Jewish traditions, but broke no specific command of Scripture and compromised no Christian tradition or ethic.

Paul's advice was to accept and observe existing social customs which are not contrary to morals and Scripture. He even proceeded to provide biblical bases to qualify and justify the observance (vv. 7–14).

3. *Paul appealed to Redemption's sequence (vv. 7–9).* The order and design of creation is reviewed as showing God's way of working out His redemptive purposes. One writer explains:

God has appointed an "order" for processing His work in advancing His redeeming, recovering, releasing works among humanity. And things happen better and they happen faster when they are on God's terms. God starts with men, *not* because men learn better or faster—indeed, we in fact tend *not* to! But this still is God's order, and He has chosen to "initiate" what I'll call "releasing life" through men; i.e., things being released to divine order because men accept their responsibilities under that order. So, we deduce: *There are no second class citizens in God's Kingdom,* but there is a creational order which God has maintained in His redemptive purposes; an order that works best when men learn to accept their responsibility as the Creator intended.[4]

4. *He also appealed to the remembrance of angels (v. 10).* The meaning of this remark, "because of the angels," at the end of verse 10 is obscure. The preposition *dia* may be better

translated "on account of." Perhaps he is saying our response may need to be conditioned "on account of" the presence of watchful angels (Luke 4:10) as heavenly representatives. Or we may need to be mindful of these spiritual beings "on account of" the punishment that was given even to angels who rebelled against authority and lost their privileged access (2 Pet. 2:4).

5. *Paul also appealed for the Corinthians to consider nature itself (vv. 13–15).* Here Paul urged them to affirm the proper distinctions between men and women as recognized in their own nature and culture. He seems to suggest that women's hair naturally grows longer than men's. It may have been that men tended to keep their hair shorter so as not to be bothered by it in their manly labors, whereas married women in that culture could care for longer hair easier because of their distinctive feminine roles and responsibilities in the home. Thus long hair was a "glory to her" and perhaps an acknowledgement of her husband's ability to provide for her.

Since matters of fashion and style are personal, how this principle finds expression in detail will vary from place to place and from age to age. The length of hair or style of suit is not so much the issue as the motive or attitude behind them. And the coiffure or clothes should modestly identify—not deny—one's gender. Certain hairstyles can be cultural symbols of gender: male hairstyle versus female hairstyle. They should be respected to maintain the clear distinction between the sexes.

    FAITH ALIVE

Is there a conflict between modesty and style in your understanding?

What about the understanding of your church? or your circle of friends?

Describe that conflict and its ramifications.

6. *Paul's final appeal was to any prevailing practice among the local churches (v. 16).* Paul is saying that there is not a definitive rule among the churches on this matter and he does not want to argue with anyone about such issues. He is more concerned about matters of faith than fashion.

To dress with decorum is a Christian principle of permanent validity, for the outward appearance reflects the inner attitude. It is this attitude of the heart that is to ultimately display God's glory. And that is never out of fashion!

1. "Head," *The Revell Bible Dictionary* (Old Tappan, NJ: Fleming H. Revell Company, 1990), 470.

2. Jack Hayford, *A Man's Starting Place* (Van Nuys, CA: Living Way Ministries, 1993), 46.

3. *Spirit-Filled Life Bible* (Nashville, TN: Thomas Nelson Publishers, 1991), 1734, "Kingdom Dynamics: Jesus and the Father Model Relationship for Marriage."

4. Hayford, 14.

Lesson 8/Proper Conduct at the Table (11:17–34)

Paul's letter of correction now addresses problems with observances of the Lord's Supper. The importance of proper conduct during this event is seen in that it is the only act of worship for which Christ gave special direction (Matt. 26:26–30). It is connected to the previous subject by the fact that both issues involved conduct in public worship.

Paul clarified the problem in verses 18–22. He had heard a report, which he had no reason to disbelieve, that what was supposed to be a celebration of Christian unity had turned into a factious display of division, insensitivity, and selfishness. In the fellowship of Christian believers all social barriers and external distinctions were to be ignored: "There is neither Jew nor Greek, there is neither slave nor free, there is neither male nor female; for you are all one in Christ Jesus" (Gal. 3:28). Race, rank, or sex were to neither hinder Christian fellowship nor grant special privileges.[1]

By the time Paul wrote 1 Corinthians, the church had developed a social setting—which they called the *agape* or *love feast*—in which they celebrated the Lord's Supper. Before observing the sacrament, they feasted on food brought by each person or family to share as an expression of fellowship and unity. As in many churches today, there were rich and poor in the congregation; some could bring plenty of food, while others had only meager fare. For the poor, this may have been the only good meal of the week.

The *agape* "love feast" should have been a delightful time of fellowship, but somehow the fruit of the spirit of love had been lost. Instead of mutually distributing the food, there developed exclusive cliques who would not share their food with others but hurriedly ate it while huddled by themselves.

And the poor—who had very little—went away hungry (11:21).

FAITH ALIVE

How did some abuse the wine intended for the Holy Communion? (v. 21)

How did Paul respond to these practices?

Could this kind of thing happen in today's church?

What should be done to prevent it?

How does your church observe the Lord's Supper? How often?

What did each of the elements of the Lord's Supper (or Communion or Eucharist) represent? (vv. 23–25)

Appreciation for the sacrament can be heightened by examining five great aspects of Paul's instruction; for the Table is to be a remembrance, an examination, a declaration, a participation, and an integration.

1. *A Memorial:* Jesus said of both the bread and the cup, "Do this in remembrance of Me" (vv. 24, 25). Like a photo of those we love, the Table is more than just a memory. Rather it becomes a present, active reminder of Jesus and His redeeming love.

But exactly what is to be remembered? Is the Lord's Supper to be a commemoration of His death or a celebration of His triumph?

Were the carnal Corinthians *feasting* while contemplating His *suffering,* or while *pondering* the power of the Cross's *provision?* Explain.

In his book *Worship His Majesty,* Jack Hayford clarifies this point: "If the celebration were focused on what Jesus finished at Calvary, then a disposition toward feasting becomes understandable. It is then imaginable, with the passage of the five years between Paul's pastorate in Corinth and his first epistle to them, that a young church newly birthed out of a Bacchanalian culture might lose their balance."[2]

2. *An Examination:* The Lord's Supper is a special, sacred time for searching our hearts and minds. Each person is commanded to "examine himself" that he or she might partake in a manner worthy of Him (v. 28). We are also promised that "if we would judge ourselves, we would not be judged" by the Lord (v. 31). Some had failed in "discerning the Lord's body," and the result was that some Corinthian saints were weak and sickly and some had already suffered premature death (v. 30).

This *discerning* examination is not to determine our worthiness for salvation; that was taken care of on the Cross. By faith in Christ's finished work we have been declared "sons of God" and "joint heirs with Christ." Let us confidently run to the Savior to renounce our sins and reaffirm our vows of commitment in the context of *celebrating the full worth of His redeeming work.* He is the Healer of our sick souls. To partake of the Lord's Supper in a *worthy* manner is "to partake with faith in His full forgiveness, full acceptance, and full power to restore, strengthen, and heal."[3]

Why is self-judgment important? (vv. 31, 32)

What was the reason judgment had already come upon some? (v. 30)

What should we do to be "acceptable" at the Table?

3. *A Declaration:* In this celebration we also "proclaim the Lord's death till He comes" (v. 26). It is a statement of anticipation of the return of Christ to finalize His redeeming work. Until that day, in the face of principalities and powers, we proclaim the triumph of His Cross! Over all our sins and failures, we proclaim the redeeming blood of Calvary! Upon all our physical problems and personal family needs, we declare the triumphant life that springs from Jesus' overcoming death.

4. *A Participation:* By faith we share a supernatural communion with the Lord in which we receive the strength and blessing of fellowship by means of His precious blood and broken body, believing His word: "Whoever eats My flesh and drinks My blood has eternal life, and I will raise him up at the last day" (John 6:54). We cannot ever fully understand how, in the Spirit, Jesus gives us His flesh to eat and His blood to drink. But we do know that when we eat and drink in faith, something special happens in the supernatural: "The cup of blessing which we bless, is it not the communion of the blood of Christ? The bread which we break, is it not the communion of the body of Christ?" (1 Cor. 10:16).

FAITH ALIVE

The Significance of Communion's Covenant. The Passover celebration was to be the last meal that Christ would share with the disciples before His death (John 16:28). It was also the setting in which He chose to transform the meaning of the cup and the bread into New Covenant thought. Now receiving the cup is a participation in the blood of Christ, and the breaking of bread is a participation in His body. The mystery involved in the covenant meal extends beyond Christ's relationship to the individual. Partakers of the covenant meal are also joined together in the body and blood of Christ. The blessings and responsibilities of the covenant are therefore extended laterally among those who partake of Christ together, as certainly as they are vertically between God and the believer in Christ.[4]

The Scriptures stress that participating in this sacrament is a serious step, therefore, "let a man examine himself" (v. 28). But also finish the verse: "and so let him eat of the bread and drink of the cup." We are called to participate in the fruit of His death, not to reenact a ritual review of Christ's sufferings on Calvary. Participating in Holy Communion is meant to release celebration, not self-flagellation. It is an occasion for sharing in the triumph of the Cross, the power of its provision, and the joy of our hope.

How often are we to partake of this Holy Communion? (v. 26)

Can this be done by individuals or families in their homes? (v. 25)

Would a holy habit of sensitive worship services in homes, with communion observed, make the Lord's presence seem more real at other times as well? Why?

FAITH ALIVE

Pastor Jack Hayford believes in a timelessness for observing this holy ordinance. " 'As often' clearly imposes no restrictions on when or where. As a pastor I rejoice in our monthly celebrations of His Table with my congregation. But I also rejoice in that thousands I have taught know and practice the celebration of His Table in their homes. In times of special challenge to faith or spiritual warfare, the bread and the cup are observed at home—'as often' as they choose.

"The only biblical requirements of righteous celebration are (1) that Jesus Himself be the central focus of the worship, and (2) that prepared hearts approach His Table reverently. That's the reason I've taught people to make their homes a place where 'as often' as the Holy Spirit prompts them, they participate at 'His Table.'"[5]

5. *An Integration:* Finally, we see a powerful anointing upon the Table of the Lord to integrate us into one body in Christ. Paul writes, "For we, *though* many, are one bread *and* one body; for we all partake of that one bread" (10:17). We are one body because we all partake of one Bread! There is a powerful integrating grace present to make and to keep us all one as we partake together of Him in faith!

1. *Spirit-Filled Life Bible* (Nashville, TN: Thomas Nelson Publishers, 1991) 1777, note on 3:28.

2. *Worship His Majesty,* by Jack W. Hayford. Copyright © 1987. Word, Inc., Dallas, TX, 190. Used with permission.

3. *Spirit-Filled Life Bible,* 1735, note on 11:27.

4. Ibid., 1733, "Kingdom Dynamics: The Significance of Communion's Covenant."

5. Jack Hayford, February, 1990 "Ministry Letter" to the listeners of LIVING WAY, a radio and television outreach of Living Way Ministries, Van Nuys, CA.

Lesson 9/*Spiritual Gifts*
(12:1–31)

Chapters 12—14 of 1 Corinthians comprise an important unit of correction and instruction about the nature and operation of special manifestations of the Spirit (Gr. *pneumatikos*, 12:1) in the local church. They are connected to the previous unit in chapter 11 as Paul continues to discuss problems relating to public worship in the church. He seeks to show "the need for varied and multiple manifestations of the Spirit (ch. 12); the need for loving and unselfish motives in these manifestations (ch. 13); and the need for self-control and for keeping an orderly, edifying manner in corporate services (ch. 14)."[1]

 FAITH ALIVE

What was Paul's purpose in giving the Corinthians instructions about spiritual gifts? (12:1)

How is ignorance about spiritual gifts manifested in some Christians' lives today?

What spiritual gifts have you seen used in your local church?

How is the Holy Spirit different from the "dumb idols" the Corinthians worshiped as pagans? (v. 2)

Would God ever motivate someone to call "Jesus accursed"? (v. 3)

What role does the Holy Spirit play in believers' affirmation of the lordship of Jesus Christ? (v. 3)

THE GIFT BEHIND THE GIFTS
(12:1–3)

The Source of spiritual gifts is yet another gift. Each diverse gift (Gr. *charismata*) is an evidence of the activity or "manifestation" (Gr. *phanerosis*) of the Holy Spirit, the active Agent of the Triune God (vv. 4, 7). These gifts may be expressed (ministered) differently, in different times, by different people, but they are the means of the Lord Jesus serving (Gr. *diakonia*) His church through the members of His body (v. 5). The results of the operation of each spiritual gift do not spring from human talent, but from God the Father, who energizes (Gr. *energemata*) each gift and each manifestation to determine the extent to which it is used (v. 6).

The "Gift behind the gifts" is the Holy Spirit, the Promise of the Father (Luke 24:49; John 14:26). The Spirit was given to influence us, to indwell us, and to empower us.

 WORD WEALTH

Another, *allos.* One besides, another of the same kind. The word shows similarities but diversities of operation and ministries. Jesus' use of *allos* for sending another Comforter equals "one besides Me and in addition to Me but one just like Me. He will do in My absence what I would do if I were physically present with you." The Spirit's coming assures continuity with what Jesus did and taught.[2]

FAITH ALIVE

Which member of the Godhead convicts us when we sin? (John 16:7, 8)

Which member of the Godhead teaches us about Jesus? (John 16:13–15)

The Holy Spirit is said to be a kind of "Divine house-guest" (John 14:16, 17; 1 Cor. 6:19). How should this influence the way we live? (See Eph. 4:25–32.)

What might we do to "quench the Spirit"? (1 Thess. 5:19) How can this be avoided? According to Jesus, what was the main purpose of the Holy Spirit's coming? (Acts 1:8)

Do you feel there are areas in your life in which you could use empowerment from the Holy Spirit? If so, what are those areas?

AT A GLANCE

Three Types of Scriptural Baptisms[3]

There are three major forms of baptism in the New Testament. Each baptism has its distinct baptizer and biblical benefit.

BAPTISM	BAPTIZER	BENEFITS
"Into Christ" Col. 3:3 Gal. 3:24–28 Rom. 6:3	Holy Spirit 1 Cor. 12:12, 13	New Birth John 3:3 2 Cor. 5:17

YOU the repentant sinner submit to the	HOLY SPIRIT who brings you into the	BODY OF CHRIST 1 Cor. 12:27 Eph. 4:4, 5
Matt. 3:11–17; Mark 1:8; Luke 3:16; John 1:31; Acts 1:5; 2:38; 10:47		
"With Water" Identification Matt. 3:11–17	The Minister	Public 1 Pet. 3:21
YOU the yielded believer submit to the	MINISTER who immerses you in	WATER Matt. 28:19 Mark 16:16 Acts 8:36–38
"With the Holy Spirit" Matt. 3:11 Acts 1:5	Jesus Christ Matt. 3:11 John 1:33	Power to Witness and Serve Luke 24:49 Acts 1:8 1 Pet. 4:10 Jude 20
YOU the obedient Christian submit to	JESUS CHRIST who baptizes you with the	HOLY SPIRIT Luke 3:16 Acts 2:4

Have you received these three types of Scriptural baptism? If so, tell about each instance:

What happened to the disciples when the promise of the baptism with the Holy Spirit (Acts 1:5, 8) was fulfilled on the day of Pentecost? (See Acts 2:1–4)

What three steps of action did Peter give to the sincere inquirers seeking more of God in Acts 2:38, 39?

Do Peter's words in Acts 2:38, 39 suggest the same resources and experience are extended to believers today as they were to the believers at the birth of the church?

What benefits and blessings are to be expected after one is baptized with the Holy Spirit? Read and summarize each of the following verses as your answer.

Luke 24:49

Acts 1:8

1 Pet. 4:10

Jude 20

Are you open to receive from the Holy Spirit the same experience as the disciples did in Ephesus? Why? (See Acts 19:6.)

Luke's terminology in describing people's experience with the Holy Spirit in Acts is fluid. He is more interested in conveying a relational dynamic than in delineating a precisely worded theology. He notes that people were "filled with the Holy Spirit" (Acts 2:4; 9:17), that "they received the Holy Spirit" (8:17), that "the Holy Spirit fell upon [them]" (10:44), and that "the Holy Spirit came upon them" (19:6).

These are all, then, essential equivalents of Jesus' promise that the church would "be baptized with the Holy Spirit" (1:5; see especially its immediate fulfillment in 2:4, which Luke describes as a filling).[4]

How to Receive the Baptism "with the Holy Spirit"

Making a clear distinction between the Holy Spirit's baptizing you *into* Christ (when you receive Him and are saved) and the Lord Jesus' baptizing you *with* the Holy Spirit (when you openly receive "the promise"—Acts 2:39—just as the early disciples did at Pentecost) is important to the thinking Christian.

• We all need to be saved from sin and baptized into Christ's body. The Holy Spirit does this. (1 Cor. 12:13)

• We all need to be baptized in the Holy Spirit to receive an overflowing of love and power for ministry. The Lord Jesus does this. (John 1:33; Acts 1:8)

The question often arises, "How do I receive this baptism, and what should I expect when I receive this fullness of the Holy Spirit?"

Answer these questions from the Bible:

What does Jesus say we should do to receive the Holy Spirit's fullness? (Luke 11:13)

Who may expect to receive the promise of Holy Spirit fullness? (Acts 2:38, 39)

What attitude ought to characterize your approach to asking for the fullness of the Holy Spirit? (Heb. 11:6)

To whom are you coming as you ask to be "baptized in the Holy Spirit?" (John 1:33)

What did Jesus say would happen when you receive the fullness or "baptism" with the Holy Spirit? (Acts 1:8)

What else can we expect to overflow our hearts when the Holy Spirit moves in increased fullness in our lives? (Rom. 5:5)

What seems to be the common denominator of the "signs" that occurred when early Christians were filled or baptized in the Holy Spirit?

Acts 2:3, 4 (signs)

Acts 10:44–46 (signs)

Acts 19:1–6 (signs)

What is the recurring sign?

What was the apostle Paul's attitude toward speaking with tongues? (1 Cor. 14:18, 39)

We do note that in *most* (but not in all) of the accounts given in the Book of Acts (as examined in the chart above), it is specifically stated that those who were baptized in the Holy Spirit *did speak in tongues*. In each of the other occasions this supernatural manifestation is implied. The one common manifestation which occurred in Acts 2 (with Jewish believers), and in Acts 10 (with Gentile believers) was that people spoke in tongues in praise to God when they were "baptized with the Holy Spirit." This phenomenon was the evidence that the *apostles themselves* experienced and the evidence that satisfied the apostles that *others* had indeed been baptized with the Holy Spirit.

While speaking in tongues may not be the *only* valid and objective manifestation of the Holy Spirit's fullness in a believer's life, it certainly is *among the initial benefits and blessings* **to be expected by those who *are* baptized with the Holy Spirit!**

Pastor Jack Hayford's irenic efforts at bridge-building in the body of Christ are evident in his book *The Beauty of Spiritual Language.* As a Pentecostal pastor, he chose to cease debating on doctrinal terms whether or not the Lord Jesus Christ had baptized a person with the Holy Spirit, and to focus on the dynamic experience instead. That removed the need for him *ever* to debate or argue again *any* doctrinal position on the subject. He explains this "liberating perspective":

> I do urge believers in Christ to welcome the Holy Spirit's fullness and to follow Jesus in His life and power! And I do hope and pray they will be receptive to and become functional in the spiritual language available to them.[5]

In short, it seems that Hayford takes the same view one finds in the Scriptures. Spirit-filled believers did speak in tongues—not so much as a *proof,* but as a *prayer* and *praise* release for *power-filled* living.

Some find the issue of "spiritual language" confusing because they have failed to consider the distinction between the personal and public use of tongues as taught in the New Testament Scriptures. They pick up on Paul's rhetorical question concerning one of the nine gifts of the Spirit, "Do all speak with tongues?" (1 Cor. 12:30), where the context implies an expected negative answer, and seek to make that a blanket answer for all circumstances. However, a more complete comparison of Paul's teaching on the value, use, and control of tongues in chapters 12 and 14 is needed for one to avoid ignorance on this important subject (12:1).

FAITH ALIVE

Did the apostle Paul speak in tongues? Why? (14:4, 14, 15, 18)

Did he encourage others to speak in tongues? Why? (14:5, 18)

What role did he see tongues providing for private praise, prayer, and worship? (14:4, 15)

What limitations did he indicate for tongues in a public meeting? (14:5, 12, 13, 19)

HOW TO RECEIVE YOUR PRAYER LANGUAGE

If you are a child of God (John 1:12, 3:3), hungry for more of God (Matt. 5:6), and willing to obey Him (Acts 5:32), you can receive by faith—right now—the gift God has promised, the release of your heavenly prayer language. (See Acts 19:1–6.)

Open yourself to more of Jesus. He is the baptizer with the Holy Spirit (John 1:33). The "Gift" of the Spirit and His fullness, and the "gifts" of the Spirit which follow, are available to sincere believers today!

Here are three simple steps which may help you receive this biblical experience:

1. *ACCEPT the gift of the Holy Spirit by faith.* Welcome the evidence of His fullness in your life based on the promises in God's Word.

"And these signs will follow those who believe: In My name they will . . . speak with new tongues" (Mark 16:17).

"For the promise is to you and to your children, and to all who are afar off, as many as the Lord our God will call" (Acts 2:39).

Accept this as a truth for you!

2. *ASK in faith.* Meet the Lord Jesus at a new dimension, as the mighty Baptizer with the Holy Spirit (John 1:33), and receive the benefits and blessings He offers:

> So I say to you, ask, and it will be given to you; seek, and you will find; knock, and it will be opened to you. For everyone who asks receives, and he who seeks finds, and to him who knocks it will be opened. If a son asks for bread from any father among you, will he give him a stone? Or if *he asks* for a fish, will he give him a serpent instead of a fish? Or if he asks for an egg, will he offer him a scorpion? If you then, being evil, know how to give good gifts to your children, how much more will *your* heavenly Father give the Holy Spirit to those who ask Him! (Luke 11:9–13)

3. *ACT out your faith.* In a childlike way, open to the miracle of spiritual language as the Spirit impresses you with the sounds and syllables to speak or sing in words of praise to your God (Acts 2:4; 1 Cor. 14:15; Eph. 5:18, 19).

Sometimes the Spirit will give you the syllabic impressions, but *you* must do the speaking or singing.

Don't try to praise God with your understanding; just lift up the sound of your voice. You must put your vocal or speech faculties into operation just as you would to speak any language. However, in this case, it is the Holy Spirit who will give you the syllables and words. It will come from your heart, not your head; from your spirit, not your soul. Your part is to speak and praise God in this new spiritual language He is giving you.

Receiving anything from God is an act of faith. Don't look for some "feeling," "anointing," or "emotional experience" before you receive and respond. We are to receive by faith; and then as we act out our faith, with thanksgiving in our hearts and praise on our lips, the evidence and the assurance will follow.

Receive this resource in the Holy Spirit today! Open yourself to new dimensions of praise and prayer in a language of the Spirit.

Some may want to pray this sample prayer of faith to receive the Gift of God and/or renew the release of their spiritual prayer language:

> *Dear Lord Jesus, I thank You that You are the Baptizer with the Holy Spirit. I **accept** the promises of Your Word personally for me. I **ask** You for this wonderful gift of the Holy Spirit, just like on the day of Pentecost. I lift up my life to You as a vessel for Your use and glory. Baptize me and fill me to overflowing with Your precious Holy Spirit! I begin now to **act** on my faith. Anoint me as I release myself to speak praises to you in this new spiritual prayer language! Amen.*[6]

SPIRITUAL GIFTS ARE SOVEREIGNLY GIVEN
(12:4–11)

"But one and the same Spirit works all these things, distributing to each one individually as He wills" (1 Cor. 12:11).

"But now God has set the members, each one of them, in the body just as He pleased" (1 Cor. 12:18).

GIFTS OF THE GODHEAD

Beyond the value of one's personal fullness in the Holy Spirit is the corporate benefit of the full operation of the "Gifts of the Godhead" to the body of Christ. Clarification concerning the source, sphere, and scope of each gift from the Trinity will transform one's thinking and strengthen his service in the kingdom of Heaven.

GIFTS OF THE FATHER

God the Father has given certain "motivational gifts" by reason of His unique creative workmanship in each human being. These gifts are described in Romans 12:3–8 and seem to be foundational to our emotional makeups and personalities. They reveal how we are "motivated" and tend to operate in life. They also explain why we respond to events as we do.

 FAITH ALIVE

Read Romans 12:1–8 before answering the following:

How submitted to God must we be if our lives are to be fulfilled and fruitful? (v. 1)

What will pollute our foundational gift or cancel its effectiveness? (v. 2)

How can we know and do the will of God? (v. 2)

How are we to think about our limitations and personality design? (vv. 3–5)

Which gift do you feel is your primary gift? (i.e., the one which "motivates" you and your unique personality more than others? (vv. 6–8)

GIFTS OF THE SON

Because the leadership gifts of apostle, prophet, evangelist, pastor, and teacher are included in this primary Corinthian passage (1 Cor. 12—14), they are often considered among the "gifts of the Spirit." It is helpful to note that these "office gifts" (first found in Eph. 4:11) are actually gifts (Gr. *domata;* Eph. 4:8) to the church by its Founder, Jesus Christ Himself. These "gifts of the Son" are placed in the church to equip "the saints for the work of the ministry, for the edifying of the body of Christ" (Eph. 4:12).

 FAITH ALIVE

Explain the place of special recognition in Scripture of the founding apostles. (Luke 6:13; Acts 1:25; 2:14; 1 Cor. 15:1–7; Eph. 2:20; Rev. 21:14)

Are there additional apostles mentioned in the continuing ministry of the church? (Acts 14:4; Romans 16:7; Eph. 4:11; 1 Thess. 1:1; 2:6)

How long were each of these five "gifts of the Son" to function in the church? (Eph. 4:11–16)

Which of these "office gifts" are prominent in the church's ministry today? Which are not? Why do you think that is?

GIFTS OF THE SPIRIT

Finally, the third of the "gifts of the Godhead" are related in 1 Corinthians 12:7–11. These *nine gifts* of the Holy Spirit (a seeming balance to the *nine fruit* of the Spirit which Paul presents in Galatians 5) are not all the *charismata* (grace gifts) that are seen in Scripture. But they are the ones which are specifically identified as being designed and distributed at the Spirit's direction "for the profit *of all*" (v. 7).

CHARISMATIC CATEGORIES

Three groups of three charismatic gifts each emerge in 1 Corinthians 12. Some have identified these three groupings as (1) discerning gifts, (2) dynamic gifts, and (3) declarative gifts.[7]

Read verses 8—11 and then indicate which gifts you would put into each category:

Discerning gifts—gifts of revelation (the power to *know*)

Dynamic gifts—gifts of power (the power to *do*)

Declarative gifts—gifts of inspired utterance (the power to *speak*)

The first grouping of these charismatic gifts of the Spirit are the **discerning gifts.** They are given to Christians to enable them *to know what to do or say* in specific situations:

> The *word of wisdom* is a spiritual utterance at a given moment *through the Spirit,* supernaturally disclosing the mind, purpose, and way of God as applied to a specific situation. The *word of knowledge* is a supernatural revelation of information pertaining to a person or an event, given for a specific purpose, usually having to do with an immediate need. . . . *Discerning of spirits* is the ability to discern the spirit world, and especially to detect the true source of circumstances or motives of people.[8]

The three **dynamic gifts** provide extraordinary powers to effect changes in the lives and circumstances of both saints and sinners.

> The gift of *faith* is a unique form of faith that goes beyond natural faith and saving faith. It supernaturally trusts and does not doubt with reference to the specific matters involved. *Gifts of healings* are those healings that God performs supernaturally *by the Spirit*. The plural suggests that as there are many sicknesses and diseases, the gift is related to many healings of many disorders. *The working of miracles* is a manifestation of power beyond the ordinary course of natural law. It is a divine enablement to do something that could not be done naturally.[9]

The third group of spiritual gifts are those through which God may declare Himself. Through these **declarative gifts** the Holy Spirit prompts men to speak forth publicly to minister "edification and exhortation and comfort" (14:3) to one another.

> *Prophecy* is a divine disclosure on behalf of the Spirit, an edifying revelation of the Spirit for the moment (14:3), a sudden insight of the Spirit,

prompting exhortation or comfort (14:3, 30). . . . *Different kinds of tongues* is the gift of speaking supernaturally in a language not known to the individual. The plural allows different forms, possibly harmonizing the known spoken languages of Acts 2:4–6 and the unknown transrational utterances in Corinthians, designed particularly for praying and singing in the Spirit, mostly for private worship (14:14–19). The *interpretation of tongues* is the gift of rendering the transrational (but not irrational) message of the Spirit meaningful to others when exercised in public. It is not the translation of a foreign language.[10]

LESSONS FROM THE HUMAN BODY
(12:14–26)

The Bible often compares the church to a human body. One of the best illustrations of this is 1 Corinthians 12:14–26 where the apostle gives an analogy from the human anatomy. He teaches an otherwise hard-to-grasp truth about the unity and diversity of the body of Christ by comparing members of the human body to gifts of the Holy Spirit.

Paul's first point of instruction was that, like the human body, the body of Christ was not one single mass, but rather many parts making up one unit or organism (vv. 12–14). Each part contributes something vital to the life and function of the whole.

 FAITH ALIVE

All Believers Are Members of the Body of Christ (12:12). The human body is an exquisite organism. Scientists cannot duplicate it or even fully understand it. It is a synthesis of many parts all working together in comprehensive whole. What affects one part of the body affects the whole. Each member of the body relates to and depends upon other parts of the body. Each contributes to the welfare of the entire body. So are all believers as members of the body of Christ.

We should function in Christ's body as the parts of the human body function in it. The amputation of a limb handicaps the entire body. There is no Christian brother whom we do not need. The word "body" (Gr. *soma*) is related to *sozo*, meaning to heal, preserve, be made whole." This clearly shows how our lives are inextricably woven together within the body of Christ, and how well-being depends upon the well-being of others (Rom. 14:7). Let us allow Christ to knit us together in His church.[11]

The second point in this anatomical analysis in chapter 12 is that no matter how different we may be as individual parts in the body (vv. 15, 16), we desperately need each other in order to function effectively as the whole (vv. 19, 21). Each member—without exception—is essential to the other (vv. 22, 24). None is unimportant nor more important than another. As with the human body, the less visible parts often require more care and honor (v. 23) by the more prominent parts. What affects one member is felt by all. If one part suffers (for example, infected tonsils), the whole body is affected (vv. 25, 26). Functional unity is only possible when the various members unselfishly "care for one another" (v. 25). And to complete this point, Paul teaches that not all members have the same gift or rank in service to the body (v. 28). That order of ministry (vv. 28–30) notwithstanding, the church will only function properly and completely when each member is manifesting his or her "charisma" with the "character" qualities of the fruit of the Spirit, of which love is the greatest (13:13).

 FAITH ALIVE

How would you compare your place in the body of Christ to a part of the human body?

In what circumstances have you felt like an important or insignificant part of the body?

Do you find it difficult to share with others the needs or deficiencies in your own life? Why?

Do you find it difficult regularly to give others compliments or to tell them you appreciate them? Why?

If another believer asked how to pray for you this week, would you be specific or general? grateful or embarrassed? Why?

Each member of the body of Christ is more than a mere container for the gift of the Spirit. He/she must be a channel for that gift to flow and a participating means for it to function. How can you show caring concern for another member of your church fellowship this week? Who would it be? When will you do it?

1. *Spirit-Filled Life Bible* (Nashville, TN: Thomas Nelson Publishers, 1991), 1736, note on 12:1.

2. Ibid., 1603, "Word Wealth: 1416 another."

3. Jack W. Hayford, "Three Types of Scriptural Baptism," unpublished notes, 1968.

4. *Spirit-Filled Life Bible*, 1620, "Introduction to Acts: The Holy Spirit at Work."

5. Jack W. Hayford, *The Beauty of Spiritual Language* (Dallas, TX: Word Publishing, 1992), 98.

6. Adapted from Max O. Flynn, "The Baptism of the Holy Spirit" (P.O. Box 1177, Greenville, NC 27835: Flynn Evangelistic Foundation, 1983).

7. John Rea, Th.D., *Layman's Commentary on the Holy Spirit* (Plainfield, NJ: Logos International, 1972), 61.

8. *Spirit-Filled Life Bible*, 1736, 1737, note on 12:8–11.

9. Ibid.

10. Ibid.

11. Ibid., 1737, "Kingdom Dynamics: All Believers Are Members of the Body of Christ."

Lesson 10/The Need for Love (13:1–13)

Love is the lubricant of the Spirit. The exercise of spiritual gifts without love will cause friction in the family of God and frustrate the purposes of God.

First Corinthians 13—a beautiful "Hymn of Love"—is best understood by remembering that it is in the middle of a section of instruction on the endowment and the exercise of spiritual gifts. Sandwiched between the need for the manifestation of spiritual gifts within the church (1 Cor. 12), and the need for self-control in their operation (1 Cor. 14), is this profound teaching on the need for loving and unselfish motivations—especially in the operation of spiritual gifts.

The context does more than just compare love with spiritual gifts. It presents illustrations of spiritual gifts in operation *with* and *without* the spiritual lubricant of love. Harold Horton, a beloved English theologian of the 1930s and 40s, has explained it in this unique fashion: "The whole of chapter thirteen deals with Gifts in the hands of Love or Love in charge of the Gifts. So are the three chapters inseparably linked. Without Love the Gifts are willful and wayward. Without the Gifts Love is unoccupied (so far as the miracle side of its manifold duties is concerned). With both Gifts and Love the Lord is able by the Spirit to give miracle-Light at its brightest and miracle-Power at its fullest for those in darkness and distress."[1]

THE VALUE OF LOVE
(13:1–3)

Without love motivating their operation, all the spiritual gifts are valueless (vv. 1–3). If love is lacking, gifts will fail to glorify God or bless men. On the other hand, the character qualities emanating from love will form a solid foundation for the charismatic operation of the Holy Spirit.

Guy Duffield and Nathaniel Van Cleave, writing in *Foundations of Pentecostal Theology,* have explained how it is possible that love is the full essence of the "fruit of the Spirit" (Gal. 5:22) and the rest of the qualities mentioned merely describe love in all its diverse dimensions: "All the virtues that follow love are really aspects of love. The flesh manifests many vile works. The Spirit manifests love which is a spiritual jewel with its eight sparkling facets. Love is the basic qualification for the ministry of gifts; it also ought to be the underlying motive for the desire of the gifts. In the vocal gifts, love makes the difference between clanging brass and heavenly music."[2]

BEHIND THE SCENES

Many different words for love are found in the Greek language, while in English we have just one. To understand this great "love chapter" we need to understand which word Paul used and the meaning behind it.

First, *eros* was the word the Greeks used for romantic or sensual love. The way the word "love" is used in the modern lyrics of popular songs or in the dialogue of soap operas and movies in most cases would be what the Greeks meant by *eros.* This erotic love is not what the Bible means when the word "love" appears in the New Testament—even when talking about the love between husbands and wives.

Next, the Greeks had a word for the mutual affection of friends and family which was used in the Bible a number of times. That word, *phileo,* describes more of a "brotherly love." It is where we get the word, "Philadelphia," the "city of brotherly love." However, neither is that the meaning Paul had in mind in this great "love chapter."

The word Paul and other New Testament writers used widely to express love (though it was used infrequently by the secular Greek writers) was the word *agape.* This special kind of "agape-love" is used to describe the characteristic actions of God and those who would seek to be godly. It is used by

Paul in 1 Corinthians 13 to express the basis of all ethical behavior.

WORD WEALTH

Love, *agape.* A word to which Christianity gave new meaning. Outside of the New Testament, it rarely occurs in existing Greek manuscripts of the period. *Agape* denotes an undefeatable benevolence and unconquerable goodwill that always seeks the highest good of the other person, no matter what he does. It is the self-giving love that gives freely without asking anything in return, and does not consider the worth of its object. *Agape* is more a love by choice than *philos,* which is love by chance; and it refers to the will rather than the emotion. *Agape* describes the unconditional love God has for the world.[3]

FAITH ALIVE

The noun *agape* or the verb *agapao* are used in the New Testament to express this highest level of love—that which is associated with God and His divine nature (1 John 4:8–10), of which we have also become partakers (2 Pet. 1:4). Review each of the following verses and describe how the word is used in each occurrence. (For instance, who is showing love? Who is receiving? Is the love conditional or unconditional?)

John 3:16

John 14:21

John 17:26

Romans 5:8

1 Cor. 16:14

1 Thess. 3:12

2 Pet. 1:7

In 1 Corinthians 13:1–3 Paul explains the value of love by comparing it to the exercise of spiritual gifts without this ethical foundation. He first evaluates the gifts of tongues and prophecy (on which he will give further instruction in ch. 14).

Some have chosen to see the term "tongues of men and of angels" as some kind of literary hyperbole. Others see the term in the context of spiritual gifts and understand *tongues of men* as referring to understandable human languages and *tongues of angels* to be Paul's reference to the unlearned spiritual languages of "tongues" when they are not identifiable languages or dialects of humans. They may literally be the languages of angelic beings.

 BEHIND THE SCENES

"... **sounding brass or a clanging cymbal.**" The deficiency of exercising the gift of tongues without love reduced its benefit to little more than pagan worship. Kenneth Chafin explains the background to this interesting reference in his commentary on 1 and 2 Corinthians: "In many of the temples there was hanging at the entrance a large cymbal. Often, as the would-be worshipers entered the temple, they struck it, causing a loud noise. Some said the noise was for the purpose of rousing the gods. By the time Paul wrote this letter, the loud "gong" which was made from striking the cymbal had become the symbol for superficial oratory. With this picture in the background, Paul is saying that without love, the finest oratory is nothing more than an empty pagan rite."[4]

 ## FAITH ALIVE

Does verse 2 actually say that love is superior to the gifts of prophecy, word of wisdom, word of knowledge, or miracle-working faith?

According to verse 3, who is not profited by philanthropy and martyrdom?

According to verse 3, is love superior to philanthropy and martyrdom, or is it the only proper motivation that makes it profitable to the philanthropist and martyr? Explain your answer.

In the same sense, does the absence of love negate the potential benefit of the exercise of spiritual gifts, which are given "for the profit *of all*"?

Can others be blessed, edified, and comforted by the exercise of spiritual gifts, but the individual being used to pass on those gifts not be "profited"? See verses 2 and 3 again before answering.

PROBING THE DEPTHS

The helpful notes in the *Serenity New Testament* (published by Thomas Nelson Publishers as a companion to 12-Step programs) offer a unique insight and application to the study of this great chapter. Commenting on verse 3 the writers say, "Paul addresses the issue of codependency long before twentieth-century psychiatrists had given it a name. He identifies the personality type that sacrifices itself completely and unsparingly for others and yet has misplaced motivation and focus for those seemingly altruistic deeds."[5]

THE VIRTUES OF LOVE
(13:4–7)

The attributes of love are defined in verses 4–7 and declared to be never-failing, compared to tongues, prophecies, and knowledge.

"Love suffers long *and* is kind" (v. 4). According to the English Bible scholar William Barclay, the Greek word used for "suffers long" (*makrothumein*) in the New Testament always has to do with patience with people rather than with circumstances."[6]

Notice that the apostle links kindness with this loving-patience toward people. Often those who are in need of being shown patience are also in need of acts of kindness.

Love is active. It is something you do. In this first attempt at illustrating the virtues of love, Paul says love can "take it" rather than "take it out" on the other guy.

"Love does not envy, love does not parade itself, is not puffed up" (v. 4) After two positive illustrations ("Love suffers long and is kind") Paul presents a series of negative examples. He begins with the twin sins of envy and pride. Envy is one of the infamous "works of the flesh" (Gal. 5:19).

PROBING THE DEPTHS

Wilbur Nelson, the long-time speaker on "The Morning Chapel Hour" radio program, has observed in his study on

1 Corinthians, *Believe and Behave,* that envy is a hurtful disposition that is jealous of any successes or accomplishments experienced by others. It seeks to harm those of whom it is jealous but finds little satisfaction, even when that harm is accomplished. Envy is totally incompatible with the love of Christ. When Christ's love fills our hearts, there is no room of envy.[7]

Verse 4 says love does not "parade itself" nor is it "puffed up." Love does not put on an air of superiority with an inflated view of our own importance. It is humble and self-effacing. Any achievements, accomplishments, or even our appearance or accumulations were made possible by our loving Heavenly Father. As Paul confronted the Corinthians in chapter 4: "What do you have that you did not receive?" (v. 7).

"Love . . . does not behave rudely, does not seek its own, is not provoked, thinks no evil" (v. 5). These thoughts would seem to be understood for people who are seeking to emulate the kind of love described to this point. God's divine nature in us will cause us to convey gracious acts toward others with kindness and forgiveness.

FAITH ALIVE

Sometimes it is helpful to consider contrasting characteristics to make the point even stronger. What would be some terms opposite of the negative character traits mentioned here in verse 6?

Rudely

Seeks its own way

Provoked

Thinks evil

When Paul says love "thinks no evil" (v. 5), he is saying that love does not keep a list of wrong or evil done. The Greek word used here (*logizomai*) is from a bookkeeping term meaning to make a calculation of something so as not to forget it. The loving person is not given to grudges and resentments. He or she will not harbor "history." Rather, the loving person will hardly notice wrong that is done to them, choosing to give the best interpretation to the intentions others.

"Love . . . does not rejoice in iniquity, but rejoices in the truth" (v. 6). Some people love to find out the shortcomings of others and spread that evil report. They are glad about the bad. These "tabloid-minded Christians" delight in having a scrap of knowledge that sets them apart from others. In a perverse way such idle talk and gossip strengthens their self-image. And to the degree their evil rumors reduce the perceived value of others, the gossipers suppose to build their own value and worth in the eyes of others.

This is not the way of *agape* love. Rather, love "rejoices in the truth" and actively advertises the good things in others. Love is the basis of the old adage, "If you don't have anything good to say about someone or something, don't say anything at all." When there has been evil or failure, rather than expose it love would seek to cover it and see it healed. Iniquity confessed is the basis of all spiritual cleansing (1 John 1:9). Rather than relate about darkness and failures, love would compel us to seek to edify and build up rather than tear down lives and reputations with our words.

"Love . . . bears all things, believes all things, hopes all things, endures all things" (v. 7). These four positive characteristics of love do not mean that love is blind to reality. Rather than reflecting a weakness with regard to reality, love projects a strength in God's ability to transform adverse circumstances. Love supports others during difficult situations. Love chooses to believe the best about others, because God can transform them. Love never gives up on people, but is quick to encourage and affirm their future "in Christ." Love extends enduring support unconditionally.

THE VICTORY OF LOVE
(13:8–13)

This final section of study on the necessary motivation of love summarily compares the imperishable nature of love and the impermanence of spiritual gifts. Footnotes in the *Spirit-Filled Life Bible* explain that "Gifts, in contrast to love, are partial, not complete (v. 9); they are temporal, not eternal (vv. 10, 11); they communicate imperfect rather than perfect knowledge (v. 12)."[8]

PROBING THE DEPTHS

Harold Horton, in his classic study in a generation past, *The Gifts of the Spirit,* has noted that "gifts by their very nature are impermanent because they are fragments of a coming Whole; but they are none the less essential for the period over which they are designed to be operative.

"Impermanence is not a fault. It is merely a necessary characteristic of some very delightful things. The gifts of the Spirit are ephemeral like the faculties of the body. But no man neglects his eyesight because of its impermanence. Rather the reverse.

"Gifts only cease in the sense that they are swallowed up in the Whole of which they are a part. It is not a bad thing but a good thing to possess NOW a part of that divine ability which we shall have forever."[9]

FAITH ALIVE

Why is love so enduring that it can be said to "never fail" or end? (See 1 John 4:16.)

Why do you feel spiritual gifts (like prophecy, tongues, and knowledge) will not be necessary in heaven?

BEHIND THE SCENES

Some have rejected the validity of speaking in tongues (Gr. *glossolalia*) by imposing a private interpretation on what Paul meant in verse 10 when he said, "When that which is perfect has come, then that which is in part will be done away." Wishing to counteract the contemporary Pentecostal/Charismatic movement, some have claimed this referred to the completion of the full canon of Scripture, rather than the completion of God's purposes in the second coming of the Lord Jesus Christ (1 Cor. 15:20–28).

Paul used two examples to illustrate our imperfect and incomplete understanding and exercise of spiritual gifts in this age. First he employed the figure of a child who is limited by immaturity. Compared to the perfection of the new creation, everything in this creation is at a child-state. Gifts will be "done away" in that day as a child is done away when be becomes a man. "The child remains though he vanishes in the man. No man slays his child or neglects him or vilifies him in entranced anticipation of the day when he will be a man!"[10]

When Paul says he has "put away childish things" (v. 11) he is not speaking in a derisive way. Rather, using the word for a baby (Gr. *nepios*, literally, "without the power of speech"), he is merely comparing the speech capacities of an infant and a man.

Second, Paul referred in verse 12 to the imperfect state of this creation by using the illustration of a mirror. In those days mirrors were not made of glass, but polished metal. These mirrors gave a rather dim reflection, but certainly not a clear image of the real thing. This illustrates the "dim" knowledge of this age. In the age to come knowledge will be complete and instantaneous.

Finally, the abiding trilogy of faith, hope, and love are denoted in verse 13, with love stated as being the victor.

FAITH ALIVE

To better understand this sometimes divisive issue, consult these clarifying verses and respond to the questions below:

When will faith give way to sight? (2 Cor. 5:6–8)

When will hope turn into experience? (Rom. 8:18–25)

Why can we say that love is eternal? (1 John 4:7–11)

This enduring virtue of love, as developed in chapter 13 of 1 Corinthians, is used to bridge the apostle's teaching from the need for the fullness of the Holy Spirit (ch. 12) to the need for self-control in its operation in the church (ch. 14). This important tie in thought is confirmed when Paul begins chapter 14 by saying, "Pursue love, and desire spiritual *gifts*" (14:1).

Contrary to the teachings of some today, love and spiritual gifts are not in competition. Rather, recognizing the value of each, they will bring the hungry believer to spiritual fulfillment and completion. Love and spiritual gifts—operating together —are surely "a more excellent way"! (12:31).

1. Harold Horton, *The Gifts of the Spirit* (Springfield, MO: Gospel Publishing House, 1934), 93.

2. Guy P. Duffield and Nathaniel M. Van Cleave, *Foundations of Pentecostal Theology* (Los Angeles, CA: L.I.F.E. Bible College at Los Angeles, Inc., 1983), 357.

3. *Spirit-Filled Life Bible* (Nashville, TN: Thomas Nelson Publishers, 1991), 1694, "Word Wealth: 5:5 love."

4. Kenneth L. Chafin, *The Communicator's Commentary: 1, 2 Corinthians*, Lloyd J. Ogilvie, Gen. Ed. (Dallas, TX: Word Publishing, 1985), 161.

5. Robert Hemfelt and Richard Fowler, *Serenity: A Companion for Twelve Step Recovery* (Nashville, TN: Thomas Nelson Publishers, 1990), 245.

6. William Barclay, *The Daily Study Bible Series, The Letters to the Corinthians* (Philadelphia, PA: The Westminster Press, 1975), 133.

7. Wilbur E. Nelson, *Believe and Behave, A Study of First Corinthians* (Nashville, TN: A Sceptre Book), 150, 151.

8. *Spirit-Filled Life Bible*, 1739, note on 13:8–13.

9. Harold Horton, *The Gifts of the Spirit*, 104, 105.

10. Ibid., 106.

Lesson 11/Guidelines for Using the Gifts
(14:1–40)

If 1 Corinthians 12 pointed out the need for spiritual manifestations to minister to the common good of the congregation in Corinth, then chapter 14 clarifies the need for self-control in those manifestations. Here Paul gives guidelines for gifted believers exercising the gifts of prophecy and tongues in public gatherings by (1) comparing their public benefits with private exercise (vv. 2–25), (2) stating their rules of operation (vv. 26–36), and (3) giving a final exhortation (vv. 37–40).[1]

THE NATURE OF TONGUES

The supernatural nature of spiritual gifts has caused some to view them as "strange," "eerie," and generally undesirable. Paul seeks to remove unnecessary fear by showing that the primary purpose of speaking in tongues—which is also called glossolalia (from *glossa*, "tongue," and *laleo*, "to speak")—is for supernatural communication with God.

Language is made up of sounds and syllables which are stimulated by the speech centers of our brains. When we speak in "unlearned languages" by the power and stimulus of the Spirit, our mind is not controlling our tongue (our means of speech and expression), but our spirit is "speak[ing] . . . to God" (14:2). Paul explained, "For if I pray in a tongue, my spirit prays, but my understanding is unfruitful" (v. 14).

THE PURPOSE OF TONGUES

At the personal or devotional level, the use of tongues can be summarized in three words: prayer, praise, and protection.

First Corinthians 14:2 says, "For he who speaks in a tongue does not speak to men but to God, for no one understands *him*; however, in the spirit he speaks mysteries."

When we speak in "other tongues," we are sharing what one has called the "sounds of the Spirit." We are making the sounds and forming the syllables as the Holy Spirit of Pentecost is prompting the material about which to pray and praise. With this Spirit-assisted praying (Rom. 8:26) we don't have to worry about the limitations of our own intellect—whether we have all the right words and ways of expressing ourself to God. Our spirit communicates with God, who is Spirit, and there is a flow of praise, prayer, and worship which is extremely natural, refreshing, and fulfilling!

 BIBLE EXTRA

Paul used three terms in verses 14 and 16 to provide indications of the purpose of tongues in his own ministry. In verse 14 he affirmed that if he prayed (*proseuchomai*) in a tongue, his spirit was actually praying to God. In verse 16 he refers to "bless[ing] with the spirit" (*eulogeo*) and "giving of thanks" (*eucharisteo*) in a means unintelligible to others. According to Paul, the devotional use of our spiritual language may include petitions to God, or praising Him for who He is, or thanking Him for what He has done.

 BEHIND THE SCENES

Pat Boone readily shares about this experience with spiritual language in his own life in his book, *A New Song*: "Like anything else, the more I've exercised my gift, the more expressive it has become in pouring out my adoration, love, gratitude—and so often, my need—to God. Whatever my spiritual feelings are—when I run out of English and find myself groping self-consciously for the way to express myself—now I find complete freedom as the Holy Spirit, in this unfettered, infinitely expressive prayer language helps me communicate directly with my heavenly Father through Jesus Christ my Lord."[2]

BIBLE EXTRA

Singing in the Spirit. In verse 15 Paul introduces the reader to the devotional exercise of "sing[ing] with the spirit."

The *Layman's Commentary on the Holy Spirit* offers added insights: "The 'psalms' were almost certainly the canonical Old Testament psalms sung to instrumental accompaniment. The 'hymns' may denote Christian compositions sung with or without music. 'Spiritual songs' (*'odais pneumatikais*) were those inspired on the spot by the Holy Spirit, unpremeditated words with unrehearsed melodies sung 'in the Spirit,' whether in tongues or in the language of the congregation . . . The origin of chants in the church before the time of Constantine may well lie in this type of 'singing in the Spirit.'"[3]

Paul told the Ephesians that all believers are in a spiritual warfare and need to "be strong in the Lord and in the power of His might" (Eph. 6:10). He went on to describe the spiritual armor we must utilize in spiritual warfare, and then added in verse 18, "praying always with all prayer and supplication in the Spirit, being watchful to this end with all perseverance and supplication for all the saints." Thus "prayer and supplication in the Spirit" is a powerful tool and weapon of protection in living the victorious Christian life.

First Corinthians 14:4 says that "he who speaks in a tongue edifies himself." We don't use this word too much in casual conversation, but *edify* means to build up, to strengthen, to fortify. Paul is saying that the Spirit-filled believer's devotional use of tongues is building a wall of protection for himself. Jude says that "praying in the Holy Spirit" is a meaningful means of "building yourselves up on your most holy faith" (v. 20). To protect ourselves from that bully, Satan, we need to build ourselves up in our spiritual man by praying in the spiritual language God makes available to those who are baptized in the Holy Spirit. This refreshing resource is a form of spiritual exercise we cannot afford to do without.

The first and foremost purpose of tongues (14:2–4) is for personal use. As a "spiritual language" it helps us speak to God in praise, prayer and for protection. The second purpose has to do with its public use as a spiritual gift for the "profit *of all*" (12:7).

Paul says he wishes all spoke with tongues (privately) (v. 5), but acknowledges that only some have the spiritual gift and then responsibility to use it in a public ministry (12:30; 14:26–28).

Paul's instructions teach three main functions of tongues in a public meeting of believers.

 FAITH ALIVE

How can we pray or praise in a spiritual language if we don't know what is being said? (Rom. 8:26)

Have you ever felt like Pat Boone and found yourself "groping self-consciously for the way to express" your deep love, gratitude and need to God? Would being able to express yourself to God in a "spiritual language" have helped? Why?

Does 14:26 describe a typical worship service in your local church? Why or why not?

Did the apostle Paul teach speaking in tongues to be a valid spiritual gift for public ministry? Why? (14:5, 26)

Which gift was preferred in public over speaking in tongues? (v. 5) Why?

What is the benefit to the church if speaking in tongues is accompanied with the gift of interpretation? (v. 5)

The exercise of the gift of tongues, with interpretation, in a public meeting was the equivalent of what gift? (vv. 3–5)

Why do you think limitations were placed on tongues (and interpretation) in a public meeting? (vv. 26–28)

Were tongues to be forbidden in a gathering of believers? (v. 39)

What place did tongues have in the private prayer life of the apostle Paul? (v. 15)

What benefit would this have had for him? (vv. 2–4; Jude 20)

Have you benefited from praying or singing "with the spirit" as Paul did? (v. 15)

How does being "filled with the spirit" involve interaction with other believers? (1 Cor. 14:26, 27; Eph. 5:18,19; Col. 3:16,17)

For Paul, these practices were meaningful and normal activities worth preserving for personal and corporate edification. They were not the strange or fanatical activities of a few "charismaniacs."

How did Paul underscore the value of tongues in his personal devotions? (v. 18)

In the church did Paul prefer to speak in a spiritual language or a known tongue? Why? (v. 19)

 BEHIND THE SCENES

The Propriety and Desirability of Prophecy. The life of the New Testament church is intended to be blessed by the presence of the gift of prophecy. As Paul states here in noting love as our <u>primary</u> pursuit, prophecy is to be welcomed for the "edification and exhortation and comfort" of the congregation—corporately and individually (v. 3). Such encouragement of each other is "prophecy," not "words" in the sense of the Bible, which uses the <u>very words</u> of God, but in the sense of human words the Holy Spirit uniquely brings to mind.

The practice of the gift of prophecy is one purpose of Holy Spirit fullness (Acts 2:17). It also fulfills Joel's prophecy (Joel 2:28) and Moses' earlier expressed hope (Num. 11:29).

The operation of the gift of prophecy is encouraged by Peter (1 Pet. 4:11), and Paul says that it is within the potential of every believer (1 Cor. 14:31). It is intended as a means of broad participation among the congregation, mutually benefiting each other with anointed, loving words of upbuilding, insight, and affirmation. Such prophecy may provide such insight that hearts are humbled in worship of God, suddenly made aware of His Spirit's knowledge of their need and readiness to answer it (1 Cor. 14:24, 25). Prophecy of this order is also a means by which <u>vision</u> and <u>expectation</u> are prompted and provided, and without which people may become passive or neglectful (1 Sam. 3:1; Prov. 29:18; Acts 2:17). There are specific guidelines for the operation of this gift, as with all gifts of the Holy Spirit, to insure that one gift not supplant the exercise of others or usurp the authority of spiritual leadership. Further, all such prophecy is subordinated to the plumb line of God's Eternal Word, the Bible—the standard by which all prophetic utterance in the church is to be judged (1 Cor. 14:26–33).[4]

But even the gift of prophecy is not without its own regulation in the worship service.

To avoid disorder or dominance of one gift over another, what restriction is placed on the use of the prophetic gift?

What if the prophet felt he couldn't restrain the Spirit's promptings? (v. 32)

What other precautions were to be observed by sensitive and spiritual people? (v. 29)

![FAITH ALIVE]

FAITH ALIVE

What feelings and attitudes have you had about spiritual gifts in the past?

How has this chapter affected your view of "tongues" and "prophecies"?

Do you feel the majority of believers in your congregation "desire spiritual *gifts*," especially prophecy and tongues? (14:1, 39) Why?

THE ROLE OF WOMEN IN THE CHURCH
(14:34–38)

Women were very active in the ministries of both Jesus and the apostle Paul. They frequently followed or traveled with them, and many were involved in their financial support. Lydia was Paul's first convert in Macedonia (Acts 16:14) and Phoebe was a helper to him and others in their ministry in

Cenchrea (Rom. 16:1, 2), the port city near Corinth. Priscilla, always mentioned with her husband Aquila, was commended by Paul as an active partner in ministry. Paul had a high regard for the value and ministry of women.

The major consideration in the context of these brief verses was the proper exercise of spiritual gifts—with decorum—in the local church. In chapter 11 Paul seemed to allow women to publicly pray and prophesy before men in the Corinthian congregation, while in this passage (14:34–38) as well as 1 Timothy 2:12 he seems to deny that same option. This apparent contradiction has been the subject of much debate.

Perhaps it would be helpful to note that the Greek word here for "women" (*gunaikes*) is also used in the singular for "wife" in 1 Corinthians 7:3, 4 and elsewhere in the New Testament. Thus the focus may be more on a husband-wife conflict than a man-woman one. Rather than muffling the ministry of women as a gender, this prohibition may be aimed against wives "taking authority" over their own husbands (Gr. *andras*, v. 35) or speaking disrespectfully to them in public. The fact that Paul goes on in verses 34 and 35 to talk of the need for their "submission" (Gr. *hupotassomai*) and to "ask their own husbands at home" if they want to learn something suggests to some scholars that some of the wives may have been disruptive during the worship services, asking questions aloud of their husbands and causing confusion.

CONCLUDING SUMMARY

This fourteenth chapter closes with an admonition, which also serves as a summary of the whole unit of thought concerning spiritual gifts: "desire earnestly to prophesy, and do not forbid to speak with tongues. Let all things be done decently and in order" (vv. 39, 40).

1. *Spirit-Filled Life Bible* (Nashville, TN: Thomas Nelson Publishers, 1991), 1740, note on 14:1–40.

2. Pat Boone, *A New Song* (Pat Boone Enterprises Inc., 9200 W. Sunset Blvd., Suite 1007, Los Angeles, CA 90069), 130.

3. John Rea, *The Holy Spirit in the Bible* (Lake Mary, FL: Creation House, 1990), 295–296.

4. *Spirit-Filled Life Bible*, 1740, "Kingdom Dynamics: The Propriety and Desirability of Prophecy."

Lesson 12/Resurrection and Reality
(15:1–58)

For the true Christian, death is not the end to life but the transition to the next. We are eternal beings. The Scriptures teach not only the immortality of the soul, but also of the body—in a resurrected, glorified form.

It is this unique doctrine of the resurrection which Christians reaffirm every Easter. For the resurrection of Jesus Christ from the dead is the cornerstone of Christianity. The Christian faith is not based primarily on the teachings of Jesus, the life of Jesus, the miracles of Jesus, the promises of Jesus, or even the death of Jesus. The Christian faith is based on all of these, culminating in the resurrection of Jesus Christ from the dead.

THE IMPORTANCE OF THE RESURRECTION
(15:1–11)

The apostle Paul taught that belief in the resurrection of Jesus Christ from the dead is essential to salvation. He told the Romans, "If you confess with your mouth the Lord Jesus and believe in your heart that God has raised Him from the dead, you will be saved" (Rom. 10:9).

The importance of the Resurrection is underscored by its being mentioned more than 100 times in the New Testament. It is the most profound and prominent point in all apostolic preaching in the primitive church. (See Acts 2:22–24, 32; 3:14, 15; 4:8–12; 5:27–32; 10:34–43; 13:26–39.)

In responding to questions he had received from saints in Corinth, Paul presented the first written account of this important doctrinal distinctive. Up to this point the Resurrection had been the focal point in the verbal proclamation of the gospel for more than a quarter century. Paul reminded the Corinthians that he himself had preached these truths to them when he was with them at the founding of their congregation (1 Cor. 15:1).

Now Paul puts in writing "the importance of the resurrection as it relates to Jesus Christ (vv. 1–11) and to Christians (vv. 12–34); he defines the nature of the resurrected body (vv. 36–49); and he reveals how the resurrection will take place (vv. 50–58)."[1] These are the fundamental truths he taught when he was with them, and the very grounds of their salvation as Christians.

This doctrine of the resurrection of the body was contrary to the teachings of the pagan intellectuals of Corinth. Their Greek mind-set allowed for an afterlife for the spirit of man, but not for the body. For them, the body was corrupt and subject to disease and decay. The thought of living forever in a resurrected, glorified body was foreign to them.

What follows in verses 3–5 is thought to be an early summary of the preaching of the apostles, presenting the gospel in a nutshell.

What were the three essential gospel elements? (vv. 3, 4)

Verses 3–5 are perhaps a brief credal form rehearsing Jesus Christ's recent, historical fulfillment of Old Testament promises. What was promised in the following Old Testament verses?

Ps. 16:10

Is. 25:8

Dan. 12:2

Hos. 6:2 and 13:14

The resurrection of Jesus was authenticated by His appearing to hundreds of witnesses. Who were they? (vv. 5–8)

Which witness is not mentioned by Paul? Why? (John 20:11–18)

What does the term "sleep" or "fallen asleep" frequently mean when applied to Christians, as in verse 6 and 1 Thessalonians 4:14? Why?

After stressing the prominence of the Resurrection in the Christian belief system versus those of the pagans around, Paul went on to underscore the proof of the Resurrection. For those early believers, the Resurrection was not necessarily an issue of faith as it is today. There were many witnesses to actual appearances of Jesus after His resurrection. All but one of those appearances occurred before His ascension.

Paul's personal confrontation with Jesus on the road to Damascus (Acts 9) some years later is graphically related in 1 Corinthians 15:8–10. He speaks of himself "born out of due time" (v. 8). The term (Gr. *ektroma*) does not mean "born late," as the sequence in the list might suggest. Instead it means he was born as an aborted fetus, incapable of sustaining life. Such a humble view of oneself gives a genuine appreciation of God's grace (v. 10) and an honest appreciation for all who preach the gospel and see souls saved (v. 11).

FAITH ALIVE

Describe how you feel about your "past" before you became a Christian?

How do you see the subtle sin of pride in your life? Is it growing or diminishing? Is it absent or prominent?

Do you daily acknowledge God's grace in your life?

Name three things for which you are thankful today.

How can you improve in showing honest appreciation for the work or ministry of others?

THE NECESSITY OF THE RESURRECTION
(15:12–19)

Apparently some of the people in the Corinthian church were denying the Resurrection (v. 12) without realizing the implications this had on their faith and future. For the sake of argument, and to show the multiplied implications of such a lie, Paul assumes the false premise that Jesus was *not* resurrected.

FAITH ALIVE

It is unclear if these doubters actually questioned Christ's resurrection, or whether or not Christians who died would be resurrected also. In challenging their doubt on this matter, Paul bluntly pointed out the consequences of their denial of either. If Christ is not risen, what four negative factors must be faced? (vv. 13–17)

1.

2.

3.

4.

The point is this: Christ died bearing our sin. If He did not rise from the dead, sin killed Him. He could not conquer it. If He could not conquer sin, we're in trouble because it will kill us, too.

Furthermore, if there is no resurrection from the dead, then all we have is the here and now. Personal pleasure alone should be our creed.

Are you a doubter? Maybe not in the Resurrection, but about God's love, or forgiveness? or about His willingness to heal your body or power to change your marriage? Write below the issues of life and death you are struggling with right now.

How does the Bible confirm God's willingness to meet you with truth and power in your circumstances? (Jer. 29:13; John 5:39)

THE ASSURANCE OF THE RESURRECTION
(15:20–28)

Against the backdrop of the negative consequences of denial of the Resurrection, Paul presents the positive consequences which flow from Christ's resurrection. Responding to the six hypothetical "*ifs*" listed in vv. 12–19, Paul proclaims the fact that "Christ is risen from the dead"! (v. 20). That fact is presented in the Greek present tense, which stressed the continuing action from a past event.

PROBING THE DEPTHS

What does Paul mean in verse 20 when he said Christ "has become the firstfruits of those who have fallen asleep"?

Why does Paul compare Christ with Adam? (v. 22) What is represented by each?

Christ's resurrected body reveals something of what kind of bodies resurrected believers will have in heaven. Review John 20 and Luke 24, then compare and contrast characteristics of the spiritual body with the natural body.

Not only does this assurance of the Resurrection confirm our faith; it certifies our forgiveness. In the Old Testament, the firstfruits of the harvest were offered to God before the rest of the harvest could be used by the people or sold in the marketplace. The first ripened grains of the harvest were brought as an offering to God on the day following the Sabbath after Passover (Lev. 23:10ff.). The careful observer will recognize that day corresponds to Resurrection Sunday! (John 19:31—20:10). Now, as Christ completes the purposes of the "firstfruits offering," everyone who follows in faith has the hope of acceptance before God as well.

In addition to Christ's fulfillment of an acceptable offering to God, Paul presents Adam as the symbol of the old earthly order, characterized by sin and death. He shows Christ to be the "second Adam," Head of the new order, characterized by righteousness and life (Rom. 5:12–21; 1 Cor. 15:45–49).

Not only does Christ's resurrection prove that God the Father accepted His atonement for our sins, it also guarantees our future. For now we can look with confident assurance toward the day of his "coming" at the second advent (vv. 23–25).

At Christ's resurrection, death was *defeated* and at His "coming" it will be *destroyed* (cf. Rev. 20:14). It is the last enemy to be conquered (v. 26) in Christ's total triumph!

WORD WEALTH

Coming, *parousia.* The technical term signifying the second advent of Jesus was never used to describe His first coming. *Parousia* originally was the official term for a visit by a person of high rank, especially a king. It was an arrival that included a permanent presence from that coming onward. The glorified Messiah's arrival will be followed by a permanent residence with His glorified people.[2]

THE NATURE OF THE RESURRECTED BODY
(15:35–58)

Among the practical questions asked Paul by the Corinthians, which prompted this epistle, appears to be: what kind of a body will a resurrected person have? This is a natural inquiry for thoughtful people who have seen human bodies maimed in life and decayed in death. Will the resurrection body be similar or distinct from the earthly body? Will we be able to recognize loved ones in their resurrected form?

PROBING THE DEPTHS

In verses 39–41 Paul suggests that the new spiritual

body is superior to the old natural body. What three comparisons does he make?

Paul then presents four attributes of the old sinful body. Read verses 42–44 and list the four attributes, clarifying their meanings in that context.

Finally, Paul shares four attributes of the new sinless body. Read verses 42–44 in several translations or versions of Scripture, and then list and amplify the meaning of each attribute.

 BIBLE EXTRA

"Although we cannot know fully the nature of a spiritual body, Christ's resurrection body reveals something of what kind of bodies resurrected believers will have. During the 40 days of postresurrection appearances, Jesus could pass for an ordinary man. He still had nail prints and He ate food, yet He could also materialize at will and pass through locked doors (see John 20, Luke 24). He had complete command over creation, as evidenced by His dominion over the fish (John 21:6–11)."[3]

Paul concludes this section by focusing on the promise, the purpose, and the power of the Resurrection's final victory. He begins in verses 50–53 with the mystery of the rapture of the church. Millions of living believers will someday reach heaven without dying. Their bodies will be miraculously transformed into glorified ones as they are transferred from earth to the presence of the Lord (see 1 Thess. 4:16–18) This was a divine secret ("mystery," v. 51) previously unrevealed to God's people.

WORD WEALTH

> **Moment,** *atomos.* Compare "atomizer" and "atomic."
> Uncut, indivisible, undissected, infinitely small. The word is a
> compound of *a,* "un," and *temnos,* "to cut in two." When used
> of time, it represents an extremely short unit of time . . . that
> cannot be divided. A second can be calibrated to one-tenth,
> one one-hundredth, and one one-thousandth of a second. But
> how do you calibrate an atomic second? Christ's return will be
> in an atomic second.[4]

The purpose of the Resurrection is given in verses 53–57.
It is highlighted by the way Paul uses the word "victory" (Gr.
nikos, a conquest or triumph) three times in this section. It is
the only place the word appears in his writings, and two of the
three are in verses he is quoting from the Old Testament.
However, this is a clear distinction in the way the Christian is
to view death from the way of other religions or philosophies.
The Law was given to weak and sinful people. Their failure to
keep its moral values entrenched the principle of sin even
more. However, the resurrection of Jesus Christ brings "victory" for each believer, because being "in Him" we can now
experience victory over sin, the Law, and death itself!

The power of the Resurrection is not in its metaphysical
transformation but in its practical equipping of believers for
service in the "work of the Lord" (v. 58). As believers, we can
now see beyond the limitations of this world and death to the
realities of heaven and eternal life. We have a powerful incen-
tive and thrilling prospects for steadfast, faithful service to
Christ in the present.

Paul concludes this important chapter by affirming that
our "labor is not in vain in the Lord" (v. 58). It produces personal fulfillment in the present, and eternal rewards for the
future.

1. *Spirit-Filled Life Bible* (Nashville, TN: Thomas Nelson Publishers, 1991), 1743,
note on 15:1–58.
2. Ibid., 1744, "Word Wealth: 15:23 coming."
3. Ibid., 1745, note on 15:45–49.
4. Ibid., "Word Wealth: 15:52 moment."

Lesson 13/Personal Conclusions
(16:1–24)

This letter concludes with a series of instructions and personal suggestions of a practical nature for both the Corinthian and the modern church. Paul shares his personal conclusions and convictions about liberality in giving, loyalty to leadership, and love for the brethren.

LIBERALITY IN GIVING
(16:1–4)

First, Paul challenges the Corinthian believers to a liberality in giving for the needy brothers and sisters in Jerusalem.

 PROBING THE DEPTHS

He had already presented this "fund raising" opportunity to the churches in what other regions? (16:1; Rom. 15:25–27)

What was the basis of his financial appeal to these Gentile churches? (Rom. 15:27)

Later on, Paul told Timothy how to instruct the wealthier members of congregations under his charge. Read this instruction in 1 Timothy 6:17–19. What was to be their attitude toward their financial resources? How should they use their relative riches?

Paul directs the Corinthians in a specific plan of giving. They were to receive weekly "collections" (Gr. *logeias*) until he arrived to arrange proper transmission and disbursement of the total. Verse 2 explains how the collections are to be made. His instructions become a prudent pattern for offerings and collections today. They are to be:

- Periodic: every seven days
- Personal: no one else can do it for you
- Proportionate: an equitable sum proportionate to your income
- Preventively: regular giving precludes the need for special appeals or pressured giving.

Someone has called this kind of giving, "GRACE Giving":

> G iving
> R egularly
> A s
> C hrist
> E nables

FAITH ALIVE

Do you believe the old adage, "God's work, done in God's way, will always have God's supply"? Why or why not?

Do you believe a lack of finances for a ministry may be a part of God's plan, or is it always an attack of Satan? Why?

May a lack of finances for a ministry occur because God's people are just not aware of the need? Why?

How can ministries share that need and encourage believers to give without seeming to be manipulative?

BEHIND THE SCENES

The collections in 1 Corinthians 16 were "offerings" for specific needs. They were not funds to be given to sustain local ministry nor to expand ministry to other areas. Many understand that the ministry of the local church is to be maintained by the congregation's "tithes and offerings." Others see tithing (10% of one's "increase") as belonging to the Old Testament, and therefore not valid as a New Testament vehicle for financial support.

Many fail to recognize that tithing actually *transcends the Law of Moses.* It is first mentioned in Genesis 14 when Abraham gave tithes to Melchizedek. Next, it is definitely a part of the Law of Moses and observed by faith by the people of the covenant (Lev. 27:30). And finally, it is affirmed by Jesus in the New Testament, not as a law but as a beginning point for accepted financial discipline for His disciples (Matt. 23:23, 24).

God has promised to reward unselfish giving: "Give, and it will be given to you: good measure, pressed down, shaken together, and running over will be put into your bosom. For with the same measure that you use, it will be measured back to you" (Luke 6:38).

Someone has elaborated on Paul's plea for benevolent giving in 1 Corinthians 16:2 by advising, "Give according to your income—lest God make your income according to your giving!"

FAITH ALIVE

Who was Melchizedek? (Gen. 14:18; Heb. 7:1–10)

How did people of the covenant "rob God"? (Mal. 3:8)

How much of the tithe was to be brought to God, and where was it to be brought? (Mal. 3:10–12)

What kind of blessings were promised to those who "proved" God in this way?

What are the "firstfruits" and how can modern believers honor God with them? (Prov. 3:9, 10)

What positive promises for generous giving can be found in Proverbs 11:24, 25?

What do you feel God is telling you for today about the spiritual blessings and practical provisions of tithing?

What is to be our attitude in giving to God? (2 Cor. 9:7)

The Scriptures command our giving to several groups of people. Review the following scriptures and place them in the proper grouping below: Prov. 14:21, 31; 19:17; Matt. 5:42; 10:42; Luke 12:33; 1 Cor. 9:7–10, 13, 14; 2 Cor. 9:7–9, 11–14; Gal. 6:10; James 2:14–16; 1 John 3:17.

Give to other Christians:

Give to the poor:

Give to support Christian workers:

Give to nonbelievers:

BIBLE EXTRA

In 2 Samuel 24:24, Araunah tried to give King David land, oxen, and other items for sacrifices, but David insisted on paying Araunah, saying that he could not present to God an offering that cost him nothing.

The heart of faith is that unless you experience some sacrifice, you have not truly given. Unless your giving costs you something that represents a portion of your very life, then it is not a living gift and will not yield a good harvest. Thus, our giving to God should have these three qualities:

First, it should be our *best.* Because God has given His best to us, we want to give our best to Him.

Second, we should give to God *first.* The first thought in our minds after we have received something should be, "How can I give a portion of this harvest to the work of the Lord?"

Third, our giving should be *generous,* flowing freely and abundantly from our heart. Jesus said, "Freely you have received, freely give" (Matt. 10:8).[1]

LOYALTY TO LEADERSHIP
(16:5–12)

After talking about the need for liberality in giving, Paul proceeds to encourage the Corinthians about loyalty to leadership. He reconfirmed his plans to personally visit them after his travels to strengthen the churches throughout Macedonia. Because he still carried a strong pastoral heart for them, he wanted to be able to spend an adequate amount of time there.

And he would not be able to do that until the Lord released him from the successful ministry he was having in Ephesus (vv. 8, 9). Perhaps after Pentecost he would be able to travel the overland route through Macedonia and visit the churches in that region on his way south to Corinth, where he could spend the winter. All of these plans were, of course, subject to the Lord's direction and change (v. 7).

In his stead, he was considering sending Timothy to visit and minister to them (v. 10). Timothy had been Paul's emissary to Corinth earlier (4:17), and they were familiar with him. However, Paul wanted to exhibit his personal loyalty for this younger coworker, and he urged them to overlook Timothy's relative youthfulness and treat him with respect (v. 11). If circumstances allowed Timothy to visit Corinth before Paul's fall visit, he urged them to support him in his ministry among them and in his later travels to meet Paul in Ephesus.

Finally, Paul underscored his personal efforts to encourage Apollos to visit Corinth and minister to them (v. 12). Earlier he had acknowledged that there were factions in the church, at least one of which was infatuated with the ministry of Apollos. Rather than exhibit envy or jealousy of this gifted leader, or to try to utilize some kind of apostolic authority over him, Paul "strongly urged him" to go and minister again in Corinth. However, Apollos felt it was not the time. He said he would go later, but for the present he would stay away, perhaps sensing the need to allow the religious rifts to heal further.

FAITH ALIVE

Who have been the people in your life who have "paved the way" for you by exhibiting personal loyalty to you and helping you make the right "contacts"?

Who should you be personally discipling or helping to find acceptance and ministry opportunities? Why?

Are you content to make plans and have God change them by circumstances or revelation?

When was the last time you know God intervened and changed your previous plans?

What would you do if a mature spiritual leader "strongly urged" you to go somewhere or assume a ministry assignment you didn't feel comfortable with?

LOVE FOR THE BRETHREN
(16:13–24)

Paul's final exhortation and greetings illustrate the genuine warmth and love he had built with those who were a part of the many churches he founded as an apostle. The word "love" appears three times in this closing section, in verses 14, 22, and 24. Lack of love was the root of much of the Corinthian division and disorder.

In verse 14, Paul again urged that the primary "fruit of the Spirit," love, be the motivating quality in all that they do. Only then could they willingly "submit" (v. 16) to the local leadership.

 BEHIND THE SCENES

Stephanas and his household were among the first converts in southern Greece and were also among the few baptized by Paul Himself (1:16). He and his family engaged in a loving ministry to others and deserved the church's obedient loyalty.

Stephanas, along with Fortunatus and Achaicus probably carried the letter written by the church at Corinth. All three were models of comfort and cheer.

Aquila and Priscilla were the husband and wife who accompanied Paul to Ephesus from Corinth and who instructed Apollo (Acts 18:18–26). Wherever they went they turned their home into a meeting place for Christians (Rom. 16:3–5).[2]

FAITH ALIVE

Who were those mentioned as being among the local leadership in Corinth?

What do we know about their lives or ministry? (vv. 15–18)

If Paul were describing your life and ministry, what would he say?

BEHIND THE SCENES

The admonition to "greet one another with a holy kiss" (v. 20) is, perhaps, a tacit reproof of their feuds and factions. The Jews were accustomed to kissing each other whenever they met. It was a token of friendship and peace, much like shaking hands in our culture. However, this "holy kiss" was more than an cultural act of affection. It was to be a holy token of mutual love between brethren, fostered by the spirit of Christ and not the culture (Rom. 16:16; 1 Pet. 5:14; 1 Thess. 5:26, and 2 Cor. 13:12).

A SOLEMN FAREWELL
(16:19–24)

The final verses, written by Paul's own hand, were a solemn farewell. He warns the believers against anyone who does not love the Lord Jesus Christ (v. 22a). And then he transliterates in Greek an Aramaic phrase, "Maranatha," which may either mean "Our Lord is come" (perhaps speaking of the Incarnation) or "Our Lord comes" (referring to the second coming of Christ). In the context of his exhortation in verse 13, "Watch, stand fast in the faith, be brave, be strong," the phrase seems to be a deep desire for Christ's return. To the world, who won't receive the Lord, He will bring condemnation (perhaps the basis of the related warning, "let him be accursed"). But to the church, His bride and servant, He will bring rewards and crowns for victories won in this life. Therefore, "O Lord, come!"

The apostle's final, handwritten remarks to the Corinthian saints confirmed God's grace and Paul's personal love for them in Christ Jesus (vv. 23, 24). In spite of the problems caused by their carnality, and even though the drain of exacting their correction had been emotionally depleting for Paul, he assured them of his sincere affection. Love covers a multitude of sins and can empower the living church of Jesus Christ down pathways of sincere service in the corrupt society of ancient Corinth or the one in which today's church lives.

1. *Living the Spirit-Filled Life* (Nashville, TN: Thomas Nelson, Publishers, 1992), daily devotional for May 5.
2. *Spirit-Filled Life Bible* (Nashville, TN: Thomas Nelson, Publishers, 1991), 1746, note on 16:15–19.